Transitional Justice in Post-Euromaidan Ukraine

STUDIES IN POLITICAL TRANSITION

Edited by Klaus Bachmann

VOLUME 7

PETER LANG
EDITION

Igor Lyubashenko

Transitional Justice in Post-Euromaidan Ukraine

Swimming Upstream

PETER LANG
EDITION

Bibliographic Information published by the Deutsche Nationalbibliothek
The Deutsche Nationalbibliothek lists this publication in the Deutsche Nationalbibliografie; detailed bibliographic data is available in the internet at http://dnb.d-nb.de.

Library of Congress Cataloging-in-Publication Data
Names: Lyubashenko, Igor, 1983- author.
Title: Transitional justice in Post-Euromaidan Ukraine : swimming upstream / Igor Lyubashenko.
Description: Frankfurt am Main : Peter Lang, 2017. | Series: Studies in political transition ; vol. 7 | Includes bibliographical references.
Identifiers: LCCN 2016050394 | ISBN 9783631671498
Subjects: LCSH: Transitional justice—Ukraine. | Ukraine—History—Euromaidan Protests, 2013-2014. | Ukraine—Politics and government—1991-
Classification: LCC KKY471 .L98 2017 | DDC 320.9477/090512—dc23 LC record available at https://lccn.loc.gov/2016050394

Publication co-financed by the Polish Ministry of Science and Higher Education core founding for statutory SWPS University of Social Sciences and Humanities, Faculty of Arts and Social Sciences, 221548/E-560/S/2016.

Reviewed by Gerhard Kemp, Professor of international criminal law, Stellenbosch University, South Africa; on the board of directors of the Institute for Justice and Reconciliation, Cape Town.

Cover illustration says: Glory to Ukraine! Glory to the heroes!
Courtesy of Prof. Klaus Bachmann

ISSN 2191-3307
ISBN 978-3-631-67149-8 (Print)
E-ISBN 978-3-653-06514-5 (E-PDF)
E-ISBN 978-3-631-71016-6 (EPUB)
E-ISBN 978-3-631-71017-3 (MOBI)
DOI 10.3726/b10638

Peter Lang Edition is an Imprint of Peter Lang GmbH.

Peter Lang – Frankfurt am Main · Bern · Bruxelles · New York · Oxford · Warszawa · Wien

This publication has been peer reviewed.

www.peterlang.com

For Maria and Zuzanna

Table of Contents

List of figures

List of abbreviations

ATO	anti-terrorist operation
CEE	Central and Eastern Europe
CCU	Constitutional Court of Ukraine
CoE	Council of Europe
CPU	Communist Party of Ukraine
DDR	disarmament, demobilization and reintegration
DPR	Donetsk People's Republic
FIDH	Worldwide Movement for Human Rights
IAP	International Advisory Panel
ICC	International Criminal Court
IDP	internally displaced person
JRC	Judicial Reform Council
KGB	Committee of State Security
LPR	Luhansk People's Republic
MP	member of parliament
NABU	National Anti-corruption Bureau of Ukraine
NACA	National Anti-corruption Agency of Ukraine
NATO	North Atlantic Treaty Organisation
NGO	non-governmental organisation
NSDC	National Security and Defence Council of Ukraine
OSCE	Organisation for Security and Cooperation in Europe
PGOU	Prosecutor General's Office of Ukraine
SCU	Supreme Court of Ukraine
UINM	Ukrainian Institute of National Memory
UN	United Nations
UPA	Ukrainian Insurgent Army
USSR	Union of the Soviet Socialist Republics

Preface

Without a doubt, justice is one of the most widely exploited notions in politics. Longing for justice is natural for human beings, although misunderstandings regarding what is just in a given situation are always associated with the risk of becoming a new bone of contention, and thus lead to new injustices. If we take into consideration the fact that the history of mankind is essentially the history of different types of conflicts, fixing the legacies of injustice can be regarded merely as one of the most essential drivers in the political development of human societies.

With the development and spread of the concept of human rights, dealing with the legacies of injustice associated with conflict has become more formal in the second half of the 20th century. Not only has it introduced a more consistent framework for an assessment of fundamental occurrences of injustice, it has also contributed to the beginnings of emancipation of policies aimed at eliminating fundamental injustice from the nation-state. Finally, human rights have become the basis of the concept of transitional justice, which in its essence suggest that not only certain deeds, but the very design of certain political regimes can be regarded as a source of injustice and deserves a more formalised, almost automatic, approach.

Although such attempts can hardly be criticised as unnecessary, there are doubts about their efficiency, understood as a movement towards the achievement of some hypothetical point in history where all injustices are remedied. As Tony Judt has pointed out: "Maybe all our museums and memorials and obligatory school trips today are not a sign that we are ready to *remember* but an indication that we feel we have done our penance and can now begin to let go and *forget*, leaving the stones to remember for us".[1] In other words, there is a risk that active policies aimed at restoring justice (here, Judt is talking about remembrance of the Holocaust) may have an unexpected side-effect in the form of forgetting the lessons of the past.

Nevertheless, policies aimed at dealing with the unjust legacies of the past, including the rich toolbox of transitional justice, are becoming more widespread in recent years, drawing more attention to both policy advocates and academia. The

1 Tony Judt, 'The "Problem of Evil" in Postwar Europe', *The New York Review of Books*, February 2008.

problem of transitional justice as an object of scientific inquiry, however, is relatively new. Yet, the literature in this field is growing and is become more extensive. This book is aimed to contribute to this field of knowledge. It is particularly devoted to one of the newest cases in terms of the implementation of transitional justice policies – Ukraine. The notorious Euromaidan protests (also known as the Revolution of Dignity) that shook the country in the end of 2013 and beginning of 2014 can be called, without exaggeration, the most significant event in the country's modern history. Although at the moment of writing these words the final outcome of the Euromaidan is far from being obvious. What is important from the perspective of this book is that it has induced a public debate on the need to deal with the past, not only the already distant Soviet one, but most interestingly – the post-1991 period. As the reader will learn, it is exactly this period of history that is regarded as the source of problems that ultimately lead to the popular uprising (and indirectly – to the events that followed: the annexation of Crimea by Russia and warfare in Donbas) and thus – the main source of injustices experienced by Ukrainians. The notions that underline Ukraine's entrance into the period of significant political change are also widely used in the public debate. For example, in his inauguration speech on 8 June 2014, the fifth president of Ukraine, Petro Poroshenko, has said:

> "The return of Ukraine to its natural, European state has been long-awaited by many generations. The dictatorship that ruled Ukraine in recent years sought to deprive us of this prospect – the people rebelled. Victorious, the Revolution of Dignity has not only changed the government. The country has changed. The people have changed. The time of inevitable positive change has come. To implement them we need first of all peace, security and unity. A real war, planned and unleashed in the Ukrainian Donbas, became an obstacle for enormous opportunities that opened for the European modernization of Ukraine after the fall of tyranny."[2]

The notions of dictatorship and the reference to the Revolution of Dignity are obviously aimed at framing the events of November 2013–February 2014 as a moment of political shift from "tyranny" to "European modernization". The speech was delivered at a time when the post-Euromaidan authorities began legal prosecutions against representatives of the former, pre-Euromaidan political elites, which are discussed in details in this book.

---

2 Text of the speech (in Ukrainian) is retrieved from the official website of the President of Ukraine: http://www.president.gov.ua/news/promova-prezidenta-ukrayini-pid-chas-ceremoniyi-inavguraciyi-32967 (accessed 20 December 2015).

The research that constitutes the basis for this book had two fundamental goals. The first one is exploratory. My primary aim was to study the scope of transitional justice policies designed in Ukraine since 2014, as well as to understand the constraints for their implementation. Due to the exploratory nature of the research, no initial hypotheses were formulated. Furthermore, transitional justice consists of numerous specific policies, each of them being an object of dedicated scientific inquiry. An analysis of each policy is rooted in existing concepts aimed at explaining the specificity of a given element of wider transitional justice. What combines these narrow policies is an obvious normative inclination, which dictates an expectation that the implementation of transitional justice in its various manifestations should support democratic institution-building.[3] Answering the question, as to whether the implementation of transitional justice policies has an impact on the political development of Ukraine in general, and whether it is an impact that supports democracy in particular, was the second goal of the project. What should be explicitly stressed, is that since the very beginning, the research was planned as an attempt to describe the implemented policies in Ukraine and assess to what extent they fit into the existing theoretical framework describing transitional justice. I had no intention to enter the theoretical debate on the essence and specificity of transitional justice, although I do believe that the analysis may be useful for further theoretical conceptualisation of the phenomenon. The analysed case of transitional justice in post-Euromaidan Ukraine may appear especially valuable from the perspective of newer tendencies in the theoretical thinking surrounding the problem which generally tends to separate from the traditionally-understood political transitions.

It should also be stressed that the conducted analysis can by no means be regarded as a basis for a comprehensive assessment of transitional justice policies in post-Euromaidan Ukraine. On the one hand, the time elapsed since the beginning of implementation allows speaking about general observable tendencies, effects and challenges. On the other hand, it is clear that a more accurate assessment of political consequences of said policies is possible only in a much longer term perspective. The analysis contained in this book includes events that took place through September 2016. Thus, the book can provide the groundwork for further research in transitional justice policies in Ukraine – both particular elements of a quite complex puzzle, and the mutual connections between them.

3 Valerie Arnould and Chandra Lekha Sriram, 'Pathways of Impact: How Transitional Justice Affects Democratic Institution-Building', *TJDI Policy Paper*, no. 1 (2014).

Furthermore, the analysis can be used as a foundation for comparative studies of the discussed case.

The book is structured as follows. The first chapter contains a theoretical and historical background for the analysis. Here, the reader will find considerations about the current state of the field of transitional justice as well as the field of research of political transition in Ukraine after the fall of the Soviet Union. Chapters two, three and four are devoted to specific policies that fit into what is generally called in the literature a traditional transitional justice toolbox: investigations and trials, vetting and historical justice. Chapter five deals with the problem that only partially fits into the category of transitional justice: attempts to deal with the consequences of the ongoing (at the moment of writing) armed conflict in Donbas. To a large extent, this chapter refers to steps that are expected to frame the post-conflict transitional justice; it also contributes to better understanding of the complexity of circumstances in which Ukrainian transitional justice policies are being designed and implemented. Chapter six also does not refer to transitional justice in the narrow sense. It provides an analysis of the links between institutional reforms implemented by Ukraine's post-Euromaidan authorities and transitional justice mechanisms, in particular vetting. Along with the edge of transitional justice in Ukraine that is targeted primarily at the post-1991 period of political development, a significant impact on the quality of transitional justice policies exerted by the fact of the state's involved in armed conflict in its territory, moving accents from purging the existing institutions to redesigning of them combined with steps to screen the personnel and replace the "unwanted element" altogether constitute an interesting specificity of Ukraine's case when compared to transitional justice policies implemented in other post-communist states. Finally, the concluding chapter of the book presents thoughts on the lessons that can be learned from the first two years of Ukraine's experience in implementation of transitional justice policies. In particular, I argue that there is no evidence supporting the thesis that the implementation of these policies provides visible effects in terms of democratisation of the country. Unlike in many Central and Eastern European countries, Ukraine's transitional justice policies are much more interrelated with everyday politics.

Acknowledgements

This book would not have come into being without the support of a number of wonderful people and institutions. First and foremost, the author would like to thank Professor Klaus Bachmann for the inspiring conversation that initiated the elaborating of the very idea to prepare this book and then to its actual implementation. Professor Bachmann was also among the first to read the manuscript – his comments were extremely valuable in preparation of the final version of the publication. It is also hard to exaggerate the significance of the opinion and comments made by the reviewer, Professor Gerhard Kemp from Stellenbosch University.

Interviews and consultations with experts were an important element of the research in this book. My special gratitude goes to Professor Volodymyr Vasylenko from the National University "Kyiv-Mohyla Academy", Stanislav Batryn, a Kyiv-based human rights activist and expert with the NGO Public Commission for the Investigation and Prevention of Human Rights Violations in Ukraine; Oleksandra Drik from the NGO Civic Lustration Committee; Markiyan Halabala, Kyiv-based lawyer and member of the Special Temporary Commission (institution engaged in the process of lustration of judges in Ukraine); Roger Duthie from the International Center for Transitional Justice. Additionally, the author expresses his gratitude to several Ukrainian civil servants who agreed to share their opinion about the implementation of some transitional justice policies in Ukraine, but to whom anonymity was promised. Special gratitude goes to Adam Reichardt, editor in chief of the *New Eastern Europe* magazine, who kindly agreed to become a language corrector and proof-reader for this book.

Ideas expressed in this book have also been discussed within the framework of two international conferences: the 21st Annual World Convention of the Association for the Study of Nationalities (New York, April 2016) and the conference organised by the College of Europe within the framework of the "Three Ukrainian Revolutions" research project (Warsaw, June 2016). Both discussions contributed the final shape of the book significantly.

Last but not least, I would like to thank the University of Social Sciences and Humanities for providing both institutional infrastructure as well as financial support for this project.

1. Introduction: Justice in times of political flux

1.1. What is transitional justice

Transitional justice is a relatively new research field. At the same time, the notion of transitional justice is used in so many different contexts and situations that there is, without any doubt, a need to start any analysis of particular cases of transitional justice policies with a clarification of terminology. In particular, two important and interrelated questions should be answered: what do we have in mind when we use the term *transition* and what makes the justice policies undertaken in the context of transitions something different from *ordinary justice*? In other words, there is a need to justify a particular case fitting into the category of transitional justice.

This chapter aims to serve that purpose, it explains the general theoretical framework allowing us to move forward with the analysis of specific transitional justice policies. I start with an explanation of what is meant by transition and what are the specific features of justice during a period of transition. Next, I put the specific case of Ukraine and it into this context, providing historical background for the analysis. Finally, the current state of affairs is presented, referring to research of Ukrainian transitional justice policies. What should be stressed here is that the subsequent subchapters are meant to provide the theoretical background, to embed the following analysis into the framework created by the existing literature, but not develop the theory of transitional justice as such.

The notion of transition reflects a dynamic nature of political organisation in human societies. The concept of transition has grown from theorizing about factors that make democracies thrive. Dankwart A. Rustow, who is considered to be one of the founding fathers of the concept, has developed it as an attempt to grasp the moment when democracies emerge rather than focus on the static analysis of relatively well-established democracies. Rustow's emphasis on the "genetic inquiry about democracy" has lead him to understand transition as a "slow evolutionary process, in which there is a deliberate decision on the part of political leaders to accept the existence of diversity in unity and, to that end, to institutionalize some crucial aspects of democratic process."[1]

1 Dankwart A. Rustow, 'Transitions to Democracy: Toward a Dynamic Model', *Comparative Politics*, Vol. 2, No. 3 (1970), 355.

What is important for further analysis is that since the inception of the concept of transition, it has been strongly related with the notion of democratization. In their seminal work on the concept of transition, Guillermo O'Donnell and Philippe C. Schmitter define it more broadly as the interval between two political regimes,[2] and thus not necessarily equivalent to democratization. The emphasis, however, on a shift from a non-democratic to a democratic political regime[3] has dominated theoretical thinking about transitions came in the following years. To a large extent, the tendency to look at transitions through the prism of democratization was strengthened by another widely cited work by Samuel P. Huntington.[4] It should be noted that Huntington's analysis of transition is quite nuanced despite the simple thesis that is brought into the title of his work. In particular, Huntington regards transition as an emanation of dynamics in the way societies are organised politically, which are described using the metaphor of a wave. According to Huntington, although we have been witnessing the expansion of the realm of democracy, there is no theoretical justification that transitions cannot happen both ways, to and from democracy.

The emphasis on democratization in the literature on transitions can be explained by the objective reality of a growing number of democracies at the end on the 20th century – the phenomenon observed and described by Huntington. The opposite trend of turning away from democracy in the beginning of the 21st century has provided ground for the criticism of the so-called "transition paradigm", which is described by Thomas Carothers as a path from non-democratic to democratic regimes.[5] Even though the path may be a two-way street, such a paradigm,

---

2 Guillermo O'Donnell and Philippe C. Schmitter, *Transition from Authoritarian Rule. Tentative Conclusions about Uncertain Democracies*, (Baltimore and London: The Johns Hopkins University Press, 1986).

3 I use Svend-Erik Skaaning's definition of political regime, which is understood as "the institutionalized set of fundamental formal and informal rules identifying the political power holders (character of the possessor(s) of ultimate decisional sovereignty) and it also regulates the appointments to the main political posts (extension and character of political rights) as well as the vertical limitations (extension and character of civil liberties) and horizontal limitations on the exercise of political power (extension and character of division of powers – control and autonomy)". Svend-Erik Skaaning, 'Political Regimes and Their Changes: A Conceptual Framework', *CDDRL Working Papers*, No. 55 (2006), 15.

4 Samuel Huntington, *The third wave. Democratization and the late twentieth century*, (Norman: University of Oklahoma Press, 1991).

5 Thomas Carothers, 'The End of the Transition Paradigm', *Journal of Democracy*, Vol. 13, No. 1 (2002).

according to Carothers, significantly limits our understanding of how and why political regimes change and what forms they may take. Following this way of thinking, some critics argue that it is much more important to focus on the past, understand why transitions happen, rather than where they lead,[6] otherwise we risk falling into the determinism of the universality of democratic change.

While critics of the "transition paradigm" do not deny the phenomenon of transition as such, they pay attention to significant problems that may affect our thinking about different phenomena taking place within the process of change in a political regime. The most important problem that is raised by the critics of "transition paradigm" can be encapsulated in the question: where does the transition end? If we accept O'Donnell's and Schmitter's definition that transition as such is a kind of threshold separating different political regimes, then where is the threshold separating transitions from "normal" periods in the history of a given country? The lack of a clear answer to these questions and the lack of a consensus in the literature on the criteria of a clearly defined "consolidation threshold" has been raised, among others, by Thomas Ambrosio,[7] who correctly noted that this problem does not refer exclusively to democracies.

The specific case of Ukraine which will be described in more detail in the following subchapter, constitutes a good example of the dilemmas of transition. In particular, since obtaining independence in 1991, the country has experienced two intensive crises (popularly called revolutions) that have altered its political regime. One can hardly predict the final outcome of a Ukrainian transition. Therefore, while it is difficult to deny the fact that the country is what Freedom House labels a "nation in transit", it is even more difficult in this case to apply the simple pattern of transition understood as change from regime A to regime B.

The approach that may help overcome the described problems of insufficient clarity regarding the direction, speed and possible final outcome of transition is the one proposed by Francis Fukuyama in his most recent fundamental two-volume work on origins of political order, political development and political decay.[8] Fukuyama continues Huntington's tradition of understanding political

6 Dejan Jović, 'Problems of Early Post-Communist Transition Theory: From *Transition from* to *Transition to*', *Politička misao*, Vol. 47, No. 5 (2010).

7 Thomas Ambrosio, 'Beyond the Transition Paradigm: A Research Agenda for Authoritarian Consolidation', *Demokratizatsiya*, Vol. 22, No. 3 (2014).

8 Francis Fukuyama, *The Origins of Political Order: From Prehuman Times to the French Revolution*, (London: Profile Books, 2012); Francis Fukuyama, *Political Order and Political Decay: From the Industrial Revolution to the Globalization of Democracy*, (London: Profile Books, 2014).

transition as a reflection of constant evolution of human societies. He proposes the concept of political development consisting of three elements: the evolution of the state (understood as an impartial state deprived of patrimony), the rule of law, and democratic accountability. Following Fukuyama's logic, political regimes emerge as a result of society's movement along these three axes. The movement here can once again be two-sided (described as development and decay), but the multi-dimensionality secures the analysis from the risk of oversimplifying the complex political phenomena by putting them on any kind of natural predetermined path, such as one between autocracy and democracy. The advantage of Fukuyama's approach is that a political development may, but not necessarily must, lead to democracy (it may lead to another form of political system as well). It also decreases the issue of "consolidation threshold", as it is focused much stronger on the problem of dynamics rather than the above-mentioned question about what makes democracies (or any other type of political regime) thrive.

The second question to be answered is why there is a need to design and implement a specific kind of justice policy in the context of political transition? What is the reason to distinguish *transitional* justice from *ordinary* justice? If we refer to the explanation of transitional justice proposed by the well-respected International Center for Transitional Justice, we will see that it "is not a 'special' kind of justice, but an approach to achieving justice in times of transition from conflict and/or state repression".[9] The concept itself has emerged "in the late 1980s and early 1990s, mainly in response to political changes in Latin America and Eastern Europe"[10] – the same phenomena that inspired Huntington to write about the earlier-mentioned "third wave of democratization". As a result, the transitional justice literature is predominantly dominated by understanding transition as regime change towards democracy. This is not surprising, if one assumes that from the perspective of goals, "transitional justice provides recognition of the rights of victims, promotes civic trust and strengthens the democratic rule of law".[11] In other words, "transition" from the perspective of the transitional justice literature has a strong normative inclination: existing literature predominantly analyses this phenomenon as a policy that should support transition from less to more liberal political regimes. As Ruti Teitel, one of the central figures in the conceptualisation of transitional justice, has stressed, "the transitional paradigm [...]

9 International Centre for Transitional Justice, 'What is transitional justice?', https://www.ictj.org/about/transitional-justice (accessed 07 March 2016).

10 Ibid.

11 Ibid.

seeks to clarify the law's relation to political development in periods of radical flux, as it demonstrates processes that reconstitute societies on a basis of political liberalization".[12]

The scope of phenomena covered by the transitional justice analysis goes beyond situations which can be called classical cases of political regime change, such as revolutions or negotiated resignation from monopolized power by an individual or a political party. In other words, transitional justice "emancipates from the bonds of paradigmatic transition".[13] One of the first fields beyond such paradigmatic transition that fell under the scrutiny of transitional justice analysts are post-conflict settlements and peacebuilding.[14] More recently, researchers began asking whether it is proper to apply the transitional justice "toolbox" to economic violence[15] and whether transitional justice contributes not only to consolidation of a certain political regime (usually a democratic one), but also to economic development and social integration.[16] As we will see further, neither of these innovations is irrelevant in the discussed case of Ukraine.

Generally, a modern understanding of transitional justice covers "the full range of processes and mechanisms associated with a society's attempts to come to terms with a legacy of large-scale past abuses".[17] This constantly growing scope of phenomena, which are analysed through the prism of a transitional justice approach, suggests that within this field the understanding of the notion of political transition moves away from the classical debate in political science. Also, it allows defining the first specific feature of political transition as it is seen from the perspective of the transitional justice approach: a **large-scale violence** that often (although not always) accompanies fundamental political changes. It is thus not the character of a changing political regime that creates the need to achieve justice in times of transition, but the existence of harm experienced by some part of a society that precedes or accompanies it. We might speak about situations

---

12 Ruti G. Teitel, *Transitional Justice*, (New York: Oxford University Press, 2000), 223.

13 Dustin N. Sharp, 'Emancipating Transitional Justice from the Bonds of the Paradigmatic Transition', *International Journal of Transitional Justice*, no. 9 (2015), 150–169.

14 See: Chandra Lekha Sriram et al. (ed.), *Transitional Justice and Peacebuilding on the Ground. Victims and Ex-Combatants*, (London and New York: Routledge, 2013).

15 See: Dustin N. Sharp (ed.), *Justice and Economic Violence in Transition*, (New York: Springer, 2014).

16 See: Pablo de Greiff and Roger Duthie (ed.), *Transitional Justice and Development. Making Connections*, (New York: Social Science Research Council, 2009).

17 United Nations, 'The Rule of Law and Transitional Justice in Conflict and Post-Conflict Societies: Report of the Secretary-General', S/2004/616, 23 August 2004, para. 8.

when violence is personal and direct (when it is clear who commits violent acts, and against whom they are targeted), as well as about situations when violence is indirect or structural (when it is built into the social structure and shows up as unequal power).[18] In both cases, the scale of violence is crucial. Although it is hardly possible to set a clear quantitative threshold that would distinguish mass-scale violence, an indicator that might be helpful for defining situations when extraordinary measures, such as transitional justice, are applicable is whether we deal with the case when "crime becomes the rule [and] no justice system can adequately cope with the fallout – least of all one in a state of transition and fragility".[19]

This brings us to the second specific feature of transitional justice: its **political nature**. Following Jon Elster's proposal, I regard transitional justice policies as situated on a continuum between purely political and purely legal motivations.[20] Transitional justice policies are thus based on legal positivism,[21] and the issue of perception of legality of both the policies and the authorities designing them should be included in the analysis. Thus, transitional justice policies are influenced by several types of interests. Wrongdoers want to avoid prosecution, victims want to obtain compensation (not necessarily a material one), and political parties want to utilize transitional justice in order to increase their share of the electorate.[22] This, in turn, means that transitional justice policies designed to address the legacy of violence are almost inevitably correlated with the risk of creating new ground for new conflicts.

These considerations provide additional arguments to apply a wide understanding of political transition as a constantly dynamic process, which may occur also on the level of informal rules, even if formal rules defining the regime remain unchanged (in other words, we may speak about transition even in a situation when there is no obvious shift from a long-lasting political order, like in the cases of transitions from communism to democracy, but when, for example, societies are changing within Carother's "gray zone", understood more or less as a permanent situation when a state has some attributes of democratic political life, but at

18 Johan Galtung, 'Violence, Peace, and Peace Research', *Journal of Peace Research*, Vol. 6, No. 3 (1969), 170–171.

19 Mark Freeman, *Necessary Evils. Amnesties and the Search for Justice*, (New York: Cambridge University Press, 2009), 18.

20 Jon Elster, *Closing the Books. Transitional Justice in Historical Perspective*, (Cambridge: Cambridge University Press, 2004), 84–89.

21 Teitel, supra n 12 at 14.

22 Elster, supra n 20 at 83.

the same time suffering serious democratic deficits). The mentioned "democracy-oriented bias" in the transitional justice literature in this context can be explained by the fact that democracies are generally better at providing conditions for striking a balance between interests of different social groups. Nevertheless, there is no reason to regard generally understood transitional justice policies as an exclusive domain of democratic political regimes.

Such a wide (and to some extent vague) understanding of transitions has been criticized for making transitional justice "merely a label that gives apparent coherence to particularized practices of conflict resolution, emanating from diverse contexts and diverse actors with diverse goals, and moreover, a label that simultaneously obscures the quite different political and moral implications of these practices".[23] Although it is not the purpose of this book to enter into theoretical debates on the essence of transitional justice, for the needs of the proposed analysis I consider the mentioned critics unnecessary, exactly because of the goal to move away from applying the mentioned "transition paradigm" and understand transition as a product of constant political development. From this perspective, a wide understanding of transition centred around the notions of large-scale violence and conflict rather than the character of political regimes, which is specific for the transitional justice literature, is justified because conflicts and their resolutions can undoubtedly be regarded as one of the important driving forces in political development.

Summing up, for the purpose of further analysis I define transitional justice as all kinds of policies that are designed to address injustices associated with large-scale violence and prevent the recurrence of violence in the context of a change in the political regime. Along with these goals, transitional justice policies are also usually aimed at strengthening the political regime that designs them. A change in the political regime, in turn, is understood as a product of a political development, which does not anticipate any "natural" political outcome. Therefore, transitional justice policies constitute a (although obviously not the only one) variable that can influence the political development of a society in the periods of extraordinarily intense changes.

1.2. Historical background: Ukraine's complex transition

One might say that during the last 25 years, Ukraine has undergone a series of several political transitions. The first and most obvious one took place in 1991.

---

23 Christine Bell, 'Transitional justice, Interdisciplinarity and the State of the "Field" or "Non-Field"', *The International Journal of Transitional Justice*, Vol. 3 (2009), 13.

It was a classic example of a negotiated transition from one of the republics constituting the Soviet Union, characterized during the last years of its existence by relatively mild authoritarianism to an independent country declaring liberal democracy as a goal of its further development. Independence along with the transformation of the political and economic systems towards liberalisation were the outcome of negotiations between local communists and forces that are described as nationalists (in fact, this group was quite diverse; "nationalism" in this context should be understood as a common denominator of aspiration to separate from the USSR). There is no consensus as to which extent it was a genuine compromise[24] or a "hijacktion" of nationalism by communists.[25] What is important from the perspective of this book is the significant level of continuity that characterizes the 1991 transition. The independence was also widely supported by the citizens – with 90.32 percent of voters supporting independence in the 1 December 1991 referendum, with a high turnout of 84.18 percent.[26] As a result, the new political regime gained strong legitimacy, as independence has never been put in doubt by the political elites, and the young state avoided significant conflicts and obtained a rather favourable environment for development.

In 1996, the constitution of Ukraine was adapted, which defined the state as a semi-presidential republic. A multi-party political system emerged in the country. However due to the lack of thoughtful electoral legislation, in particular the virtually unregulated issue of financing political parties, the latter quickly became dependent on the emerging large business class. An active role in this process was played by former communist elites who adapted their networks of contacts to the new realities and used them to assure personal benefits – as owners and managers of the privatized economy. As a result, a specific hybrid political system began taking shape in the mid-1990s, often described as the "oligarchic democracy".[27] Its main defining feature is a close and mutually beneficial relationship between the political elites and large businesses. Due to the existence of multiple business-political groups (so-called "clans"), a significant level of pluralism was created. Yet,

---

24 See: Andrew Wilson, *The Ukrainians: Unexpected Nation,* (New Haven and London: Yale University Press, 2002).

25 See: Alexander J. Motyl, *Dilemmas of Independence: Ukraine after Totalitarianism,* (New York: Council of Foreign Relations Press, 1993).

26 Documents available at the official web portal of the State Archival Service of Ukraine: http://www.archives.gov.ua/Sections/15r-V_Ref/index.php?11.

27 Sławomir Matuszak, *The Oligarchic Democracy. The influence of business groups on Ukrainian politics* (Warsaw: Centre for Eastern Studies, 2012).

the political significance of the electorate remained limited. In such a system, elections serve primarily as a means to legitimize power but lose their function as a tool guaranteeing accountability of the political elites. One of the most important issues from the perspective of this analysis is the fact that the political regime that emerged in Ukraine in the 1990s and early 2000s was a combination of weak formal and strong informal rules identifying the real power holders and the limitations to their power. Corruption, which became an intrinsic feature of the system, can be regarded as a significant indicator showing the importance of the informal rules governing Ukraine's political system, which was accompanied by highly politicized justice.[28]

The Ukrainian "oligarchic democracy" flourished under President Leonid Kuchma (1994–2004) who played the specific role of arbiter for the oligarchic "clans" competing among each other. A lack of accountability became one of the main reasons for the political crisis in 2004 – the Orange Revolution. Mass protests were triggered after the authorities attempted to falsify the presidential elections in favour of Viktor Yanukovych, who was seen as Kuchma's successor. However, the main reasons for the protests can be found in a wide dissatisfaction with the social and economic situation, as well as high levels of corruption and patrimonialization of the state. The protests ended peacefully when an agreement between the authorities and the opposition to repeat the second round of voting was reached, which eventually brought victory to Viktor Yushchenko.

Some regard the Orange Revolution as Ukraine's second transition.[29] The main argument that supports this thesis is the fact that the authorities agreed to repeat the election under the condition that the constitution is amended. The reform of 2004 led Ukraine to become a parliamentary republic, thus limiting the powers of the newly-elected president. The crisis also brought a reshuffle in the relative power among the different "clans" and politicians representing them. Yet, the informal system of "oligarchic democracy" did not change its essence. In other words, the change of the formal "rules of the game", in particular the transfer of the main centre of power from the president to prime minister, did not overcome the inertia of the informal rules. This in fact supports the thesis about the importance of the informal rules. Moreover, President Yushchenko, deprived of many rights by the constitutional reform, failed to become an arbiter as effective as his

---

28 See: Maria Popova, *Politicized Justice in Emerging Democracies. A Study of Courts in Russia and Ukraine*, (New York: Cambridge University Press, 2014).

29 Geir Flikke, 'Pacts, Parties and Elite Struggle: Ukraine's Troubled Post-Orange Transition', *Europe-Asia Studies*, Vol. 60, No. 3 (2008).

predecessor. This led Ukraine to a state of long-term institutional chaos. As a result, Viktor Yanukovych, the main loser of the Orange Revolution, was successful in the presidential election of 2010.[30]

Under the presidency of Yanukovych, Ukraine faced an unprecedented level of concentration of power by one political party – the pro-presidential Party of Regions. This became possible thanks in part to the undoing of the 2004 constitutional reform per the decision of the Constitutional Court in 2010. This occurrence can also be regarded as a new transition between political regimes. Furthermore, the legality of the move was doubtful and thus paved the way for notions of usurpation of power by Viktor Yanukovych. Along with the new modification of the formal "rules of the game", the informal system of oligarchic "clans" faced its own unprecedented problem – the president and his close allies (characterized as "the family") attempted to build their own oligarchic "clan", instead of playing the traditional role of arbiter.[31] This attempt also resulted in an unprecedented growth of corruption. In fact, abuse and fraud in financial, legal and moral terms became so widespread it began encumbering the whole state.[32] The attempt to concentrate both political and economic power in one's hands, along with the deep dissatisfaction of a significant part of population with the developments in the country, led to a new crisis between November 2013 and February 2014, known as the Euromaidan or the Revolution of Dignity. This event indicates the most recent of Ukraine's political transitions (at least as of the writing of this book). The Euromaidan protest as well as its aftermath is crucial for this book as only after these events the authorities of Ukraine have initiated a whole spectre of transitional justice mechanisms.

The Euromaidan protests started on 21 November 2013 as a demonstration against the government's decision not to sign the Association Agreement with the European Union – a treaty that provides ground for Ukraine's gradual economic integration with the EU's Single Market and closer political linkages between

---

30 For more information about the Orange Revolution see: Andrew Wilson, *Ukraine's Orange Revolution*, (New Haven: Yale University Press, 2005); Anders Aslund and Michael McFaul (ed.), *Revolution in Orange: The Origins of Ukraine's Democratic Breakthrough*, (Washington D.C.: Carnegie Endowment for International Peace, 2006).

31 Matuszak, supra n 27 at 41–50.

32 A good insight into the problem is presented by a journalistic investigation by Sergii Leshchenko, basing on documents found in Viktor Yanukovych's residence in Mezhyhirya after his escape to Russia. See: Sergii Leshchenko, *Mezhyhirskyy syndrome. Diagnoz vladi Yanukovycha*, (Kyiv: Brayt Buks, 2014).

both sides. At the initial phase, the protest was dominated by young people presenting pro-European attitudes. During the night between 29 and 30 November, the authorities used violent force against the protesters for the first time. The demonstration was dispersed by *Berkut* special police units. The consequence of this occurrence was opposite to the expectations of the authorities. The use of force motivated even much more people to join the protest. As a result, a permanent camp was established in the centre of Kyiv. At this point, the motivation of the protesters had evolved from being a pro-European movement to a more anti-governmental one with anti-establishment sentiments. Both sides of the three-months-long confrontation had radicalised themselves, since the start of December 2013. On 16 January 2014, a package of so-called "dictatorial laws" was adopted by the Ukrainian parliament, limiting the legal possibilities to organise civic protests and introducing censorship-like policies online and reducing the rights of the independent mass media. This led to a new wave of violent clashes between the protesters and the police.

The resignation of then Prime Minister Mykola Azarov failed to relieve tension. The protesters demanded the cancellation of the "dictatorial laws", an unconditional stop of prosecution against anyone arrested for their participation in the protests, a return to the 2004 version of the constitution as well as the resignation of President Yanukovych himself. The authorities agreed only to cancel the "dictatorial laws". On 18 February 2014, protesters organised a march to the parliament where the return to 2004 version of the constitution was to be voted on. The parliament's chairman however refused to register the issue on the parliament agenda, which triggered the final wave of the most violent clashes which lasted till 21 February and costed the lives of around 100 people.

In order to put an end to the bloodshed and find a political solution to the crisis, a mediation mission of three EU foreign ministers (Radosław Sikorski, Frank-Walter Steinmeier and Laurent Fabius) as well as the Russian ombudsman Vladimir Lukin came to Kyiv. The international mediators certified an agreement signed on 21 February 2014 between President Yanukovych and leaders of the Ukrainian opposition. The main points of the agreement included a return to the 2004 Constitution within 48 hours, the creation of a new national unity governmental coalition and a new constitution by September 2014. It also stipulated early presidential elections no later than December 2014 and an accurate investigation of the violence that happened since the beginning of the unrest to be conducted under the monitoring of the authorities, the opposition and the Council of Europe.

This agreement could be regarded as an argument that Ukraine's post-Euromaidan transition bears signs of one being negotiated. However, this statement is far from being obvious since Yanukovych fled to Russia the following day, and thus not fulfilling any of the points in the agreement. Upon the escape of the president, the parliament, which was elected two years prior to the outbreak of the crisis, took responsibility for the situation in the country in order to keep the situation under control. Among the first decisions made was to delegitimise the 2010 verdict of the Constitutional Court, restoring the 2004 version of the constitution and thus bringing back the parliamentary republic. An interim government under Arseniy Yatsenyuk as prime minister was formed on 27 February 2014.[33] A date for early presidential elections was set for 26 May 2014, which were won by Petro Poroshenko. On 26 October 2014, early parliamentary elections took place, thus ending the process of renewing the central state institutions in the post-Euromaidan Ukraine. Five parliamentary fractions made up the new governing coalition: Petro Poroshenko's Block (BPP), Arseniy Yatsenyuk's People's Front, Yulia Tymoshenko's *Batkivshchyna* (Fatherland), the liberal *Samopomich* (self-reliance) party and the somewhat populist Radical Party. Arseniy Yatsenyuk kept the position of prime minister and remained in this position until April 2016.

Almost immediately after the end of the Euromaidan protests, strong centrifugal tendencies were initiated in Ukraine supported by the Russian Federation. On 18 March 2014 the process of the annexation of Crimea by Russia was finalized. In parallel, separatist movements began taking hold in the Donbas region (covering Donetsk and Luhansk oblasts of Ukraine), escalating into full-blown conflict by the summer of 2014. On 11 May 2014, unconstitutional referendums[34] took place in the territories captured by the separatists, which later announced their independence as self-proclaimed "people's republics" of Donetsk and Luhansk.

Attempts have been made to negotiate a peaceful resolution to the conflict. The first ceasefire was negotiated in Minsk, Belarus on 5 September 2014, but failed after several days. A second ceasefire, negotiated on 12 February 2015, appeared to be more effective, but resulted in the lowering of intensity of violence rather than a complete end to it. The relative calmness, although not total peace was achieved in September 2015. The conflict brought thousands of killed

---

33 For more information about the Euromaidan protest see: Igor Lyubashenko, 'Euromaidan: From the students' protest to mass uprising', in *The Maidan Uprising, Separatism and Foreign Intervention. Ukraine's complex transition*, ed. Klaus Bachmann and Igor Lyubashenko (Frankfurt am Main: Peter Lang Edition, 2014), 61–85.

34 The constitution of Ukraine does not foresee the institution of a regional referendum. Furthermore, according to art. 73 of the constitution, the issue of change of the territory of Ukraine can only be a matter of nationwide referendum.

and many more injured,[35] both among the military and the civilians, as well as millions of internally displaced persons. The roots of the conflict as well as the legacy of it illustrate an additional important constraint for Ukraine's post-Euromaidan political development. In particular, the violence that took place during the conflict created a field for a completely new, somehow unexpected use of transitional justice mechanisms.

In conclusion, Ukraine's experience of transition between political regimes is extremely rich, mainly due to the coincidence of the 1991 regime change with the processes of both state- and nation-building. Nevertheless, Ukraine is to a large extent absent from the literature on political transitions. Due to complexity and irregularity of the post-1991 political developments, Ukraine somehow stands out from comparative studies devoted to post-communist countries, which focus mainly on Central and Eastern European states. At most, different research has put accents on different aspects of politics in independent Ukraine: the weakness of political parties,[36] the ill-designed constitutional framework,[37] and the prevalence of non-transparent "virtual politics"[38] that hides real interests of key political players, to name the most significant ones.

There are thus at least two important features that distinguish Ukraine's post-communist political development from the general pattern observed in most Central European states and thus create a completely different context for the implementation of transitional justice policies. The first is an irregularity of the direction and speed of change. One may argue whether the dates of 2004, 2010 and 2014 should be regarded as separate transitions. What is obvious, however, is that while neither of these dates mark a change so fundamental as the one that took place in 1991, each of them has brought a significant modification of the political regime in Ukraine. These "transformation of the political regime zigzags"[39] correspond with the understanding of the nature of political transition presented in the previous subchapter, which could take the form of changes within the "gray zone", between autocracy and democracy. Furthermore, at the

---

35 These problems are discussed in detail in chapter 5.

36 Taras Kuzio, 'Impediments to the Emergence of Political Parties in Ukraine', *Politics*, vol. 34 no. 4 (2014).

37 Kataryna Wolczuk, *The Moulding of Ukraine: The Constitutional Politics of State Formation*, (Budapest: Central European University Press, 2001).

38 Andrew Wilson, *Virtual Politics: Faking Democracy in the Post-Soviet World*, (New Haven, London: Yale University Press, 2005).

39 Yuri Matsiyevski, 'Change, Transition, or Cycle. The Dynamics of Ukraine's Political Regime in 2004–2010', *Russian Politics and Law*, Vol. 49, No. 5 (2011), 17.

time of writing it is obviously too early to speak about a final outcome in the transition that has started in 2014. The second feature is defined by the large-scale violence that the Ukrainian society has faced since the end of 2013, both in relations between the society and the authorities and in relations between different groups of the society itself (combined with international interference). In this regard, the Ukrainian experience is much closer (although far from being similar) to that of the former Yugoslav republics.

1.3. Transitional justice in Ukraine

As mentioned above, the experience of transitions in post-communist states became one of the main inspirations for the development of transitional justice theory. As a result, the literature on transitional justice in post-communist countries is quite extensive. Most of the studies are devoted to the policies of lustration and criminal prosecutions of former communist officials, covering also the issue of historic policies.[40] Quite often, these policies are characterized as nearly fundamental for post-communist democratic regimes. Their complexity implies on explanation of both which factors constrain the policies and how the policies impact politics in a given country. Therefore, transitional justice policies have been studied as both a dependent variable (what determines the specific shapes of these policies in particular countries?)[41] and an independent variable (to explain whether implementation of transitional justice mechanisms was supportive for democratic consolidations).[42] With the exception of the Baltic states,[43] there are only occasional analyses focusing on specific situations of former Soviet republics.[44] The

40 For example: Natalia Letki, 'Lustration and Democratisation in East-Central Europe', *Europe-Asia Studies*, Vol. 54, No. 4 (2002); Lavinia Stan and Nadya Nedelsky (ed.), *Post-Communist Transitional Justice. Lessons from Twenty-Five Years of Experience* (New York: Cambridge University Press, 2015).

41 A good overview of literature: Lavinia Stan, 'Determinants of Post-Communist Transitional Justice: An Overview', paper prepared for the Global Challenges Conference "Justice and Imagination: Building Peace in Post-Conflict Societies", Mount Holyoke College, 28 February–1 March 2014.

42 Cynthia M. Horne, 'The Impact of Lustration on Democratization in Postcommunist Countries', *The International Journal of Transitional Justice*, Vol. 8 (2014).

43 Eva-Clarita Pettai, Vello Pettai, *Transitional and Retrospective Justice in the Baltic States*, (Cambridge: Cambridge University Press, 2015).

44 For example: Kora Andrieu, 'An Unfinished Business: Transitional Justice and Democratization in Post-Soviet Russia', *The International journal of Transitional Justice*, Vol. 5 (2011).

reason for that is quite simple: until very recently, the former Soviet republics have not implemented transitional justice policies. In 2011, Georgia became the first to adopt a lustration law (the so-called Freedom Charter), which was aimed at dealing with the legacy of its Soviet past.[45] Ukraine has joined the club only in 2014, in the aftermath of the discussed Euromaidan protests.

The fact that the Soviet legacy constitutes a significant burden to Ukraine's post-1991 political development seems to be a general consensus. According to Paul J. D'Anieri, for example, the main root of Ukraine's problems is the political and institutional legacy of the Soviet Union, in particular the lack of a tradition of genuine respect to the principle of division of powers and state control over economy (which has become the foundation for widespread corruption).[46] Anders Aslund's analysis conducted already after the Euromaidan looks very similar:

> "Ukraine's fundamental problem is that it did not experience any clear break from the communist system. Its tardy transition to a market economy bred pervasive corruption by giving the old elite ample opportunities to transform their power into personal wealth. They did so with great success, to the detriment of society, building a rent-seeking oligarchy that was never effectively challenged during Ukraine's 23 years of independence from the Soviet Union".[47]

Despite these widely discussed connections between the Soviet legacy and the post-1991 problems, and despite the fact that Ukraine was one of the republics who suffered the most from the communist rule, the state has not implemented any comprehensive transitional justice policy after gaining independence and the most fundamental change of the political regime in 1991 (although there were several steps which would fit the category of so-called historical justice – they are described in chapter four). On the contrary, Ukraine is usually presented as an example of "'*de facto* amnesty', a situation in which perpetrators of human rights violations enjoy an amnesty by virtue of the state decision not to address past abuses."[48] Indeed, the most significant act that can be regarded as an example of

---

45 Margarita Antidze, 'Pro-Western Georgia to get rid of Soviet symbols', *Reuters*, 31.05.2011, http://www.reuters.com/article/uk-georgia-soviet-idUSLNE74U05Z20110531 (accessed 29 June 2016).

46 Paul D'Anieri, *Understanding Ukrainian Politics. Power, Politics and Institutional Design*, (New York, London: M.E. Sharpe, 2007), 13–14.

47 Anders Aslund, *Ukraine. What Went Wrong and How to Fix It*, (Washington D.C.: Peterson Institute for International Economics, 2015), 4.

48 Tricia D. Olsen, Leigh A. Payne, Andrew G. Reiter, *Transitional Justice in Balance. Comparing processes, weighing efficacy*, (Washington D.C.: United States Institute of Peace Press, 2010), 40.

transitional justice policy was a ban of the Communist Party of the Soviet Union in 1991. It did not prevent the Constitutional Court of Ukraine from allowing the renewed Communist Party of Ukraine to be registered and participate in the political process since 1993, basing on the assumption that the latter was not an assignee of the former. According to Mykola Ryabchuk, the ban of the Communist Party was a "symbolic gesture, not a real output – a kind of simulacrum, public burning of an empty and mouldering skin of a snake, aimed at drawing attention away from the real movements and reincarnations of post-communist 'snakes' – the party, KGB and other nomenklatura".[49] As a result, Ukraine has not developed effective mechanisms of cleansing its politics from the members of the Soviet elite. In fact, there was neither political will among the elites nor sufficient public pressure to do so. Ultimately, the compromise between the communists and nationalists *de facto* gave power to the former *nomenklatura*. According to some historians this move helped avoid the outbreak of a major conflict in the beginning of the 1990s – at that time, Ukraine faced the problem of a "lack of patriotic and experienced cadres, characterized by the pragmatic, large-scale thinking and understanding of the real situation".[50] The attitude towards the problem of dealing with the communist past was probably best expressed by the second president of Ukraine, Leonid Kuchma:

> "I think, we have done well, when, unlike Central European and Baltic states, we allowed the communists to register their party under the former name. They want to be communists? Let them be! At least we cannot be accused of leaving no choice for the significant part of our population."[51]

The situation has changed after 2014, when not only the modification of the political regime took place, but also for the first time in recent history the country had to face the legacy of political violence: first the killings of Euromaidan protesters and then victims of the armed conflict in the east of Ukraine. As a result, a whole number of new legislations was passed, whose predominant aim was to address past abuses, de-legitimize the former president's rule, bolster power, legitimacy and public support for the new government and punish key supporters of the *ancien regime*. In other words, when Ukraine finally began implementing transitional justice policies they were targeted predominantly at the period that followed the fall of communism. More "traditional" (from the perspective of

---

49 Mykola Ryabchuk, *Ulyublenyy pistolet Pani Simpson. Khronika pomaranchevoyi porazky*, (Kyiv: K.I.S., 2009), 10.

50 Roman Shporlyuk, *U poshukah maybutnioho chasu*, (Kyiv: Hrani-T, 2010), 21.

51 Leonid Kuchma, *Ukrayina – ne Rossiya*, (Moscow: Vremya, 2003), 123.

CEE) elements of transitional justice with the edge aimed against pre-1991 political establishment were also there, but they did not dominate the transitional justice agenda. Moreover, one of the policies is aimed at dealing with the legacy of the ongoing conflict in Donbas. All in all, after having no transitional justice policies since gaining independence, Ukraine experienced a kind of "big bang" in this sphere, additionally opening a new field for research for anyone interested in the topic of transitional justice. This book aims to be the first steps to start filling the gap that has emerged.

The following chapters of the book refer directly to the research questions that constitute the basis for the research: (1) what is the scope of transitional justice policies designed and implemented in Ukraine and (2) what is the impact of these policies on the political development of the country? The chapters are devoted to five separate policies that fit into the defined framework of transitional justice: investigations and trials, vetting, historical justice, dealing with the legacy of the Donbas conflict and linkage between institutional reforms and transitional justice. The analysis of each policy includes a more detailed theoretical background which refers to the existing literature on the discussed problems, a description of abuses addressed by the policies, perception of them by the society and the public debate referring to them, the design of implemented policies, effects and constraints for the implementation of these policies. Chapter 5 stands out slightly from this scheme, due to the fact that it is devoted to transitional justice policy, which at the moment of writing the book was still *in statu nascendi*. Therefore, much more attention is devoted to determinants of design and implementation of transitional justice mechanisms aimed at dealing with the legacy of the warfare in Donbas. Also chapter 6 does not deal with a comprehensive transitional justice policy but rather with the supplementary steps that are aimed at reinforcing the effects of the policies analysed in chapters 2–5. The whole is summed up by the conclusion on the impact of the discussed policies on the political development of Ukraine. By applying the proposed analysis of political transition through the prism of an open-ended process of political development, the aim is to eliminate the risk of falling into the already-mentioned determinism of "transition paradigm" and to regard transitional justice policies as the outcome of a specific political situation and at the same time as a variable that may have an impact on the society's further development without predetermining the exact outcome of the development (in the particular case of Ukraine, covered by this book without anticipating that the country will follow the steps of political development of its CEE neighbours and eventually become a western-like liberal democracy).

Therefore, Geoff Dancy's proposal to think in terms of impact assessment rather than evaluation of transitional justice policies is especially valuable for the purposes of this book. According to him: "evaluation implies judgement of the goal-reaching capabilities of mechanisms and requires two basic activities: first, selection of a set of appropriate objectives toward which a body aims [...] and, second, review and judgement of a body's performance based on those criteria".[52] Impact assessment, on the contrary, allows to keep analytical distance from the values declared by the political regime that introduces transitional justice policies and regard a lack of achievement of declared goals as significant for the political development (or political decay) of the country. This approach also allows for avoiding the dangers related with the normative inclinations of transitional justice policies. In this book, the normative aspects of transitional situation are regarded as criteria that set up basic legal standards relevant to transitional policies in general and transitional justice in particular.[53] In other words, values proclaimed by the incoming regime starting implementation of transitional justice policies constitute a kind of "normative anchor" allowing to conduct an impact assessment of these policies.

52 Geoff Dancy, 'Impact Assessment, Not Evaluation: Defining a Limited Role for Positivism in the Study of Transitional Justice', *The International Journal of Transitional Justice*, vol. 4 (2010), 359.

53 Alexander Mayer-Rieckh, 'On Preventing Abuse: Vetting and Other Transitional Reforms,' in *Justice as Prevention. Vetting Public Employees in Transitional Societies*, ed. Alexander Mayer-Riekh and Pablo de Greiff, (New York: Social Science Research Cancel, 2007), 504.

2. Investigations and trials

2.1. Theoretical background

"Bandits will go to jail!"[1] – This was probably one of the best-remembered slogans used by Viktor Yushchenko in his notorious presidential campaign in 2004 before the Orange Revolution. The slogan referred not to any particular person, but to the generally understood political elites who mismanaged the country and finally tried to "steal" the people's voices in the presidential election. An average voter could have imagined almost anyone in the role of a "bandit" – a former president, one of the presidential candidates, or some anonymous official who tried to extort a bribe from that very same average voter. The perspective to punish this bandit seemed to be very attractive. Nevertheless, it remained nothing more than an electoral slogan.

Blaming the predecessors for all that is wrong is common practice in politics, especially if the government changes regularly. It is also quite common to hear in everyday discussions that the government (and even the whole political elite) is made up of "bandits". Usually, these are nothing more than empty catchphrases used in political competition. They are impersonal accusations that do not bear any legal consequences. Of course, the widespread use of such slogans provides no evidence of maturity in a public debate. Nevertheless, the notion of "punishing" politicians has entered our thinking around one of the essential features of a democratic political process – accountability. "Punishment" in this case has a political nature and takes the form of not re-electing the ones who govern the country if, in the opinion of the voters, there is a basis to blame them for a poor state of affairs in the country. Sometimes, however, politicians actually do break the law. In such cases political accountability takes legal form. This process is much more complicated in a state that is in the midst of a political transition.

Wherever the principle of the rule of law is in force, investigations and trials may be regarded as mechanisms that are the least susceptible to political pressure – if representatives of the authorities break the law, an investigation, trial and eventual sentence should be a natural consequence. Therefore, they are usually regarded as the least controversial mechanisms of transitional justice. However, when the rules identifying political power holders and limitations to exercise power change, one can expect that the incoming regime may have a motivation

---

1 In Ukrainian: *Бандити сидітимуть у тюрмах!*

to go beyond impersonal blaming of predecessors and actually initiate investigations targeted against the representatives of the *ancien regime*, especially in a situation when the transition is from a less to more liberal regime. Whether there is ground to conduct such actions depends generally on two issues. The first is whether the law has actually been broken. Obviously, it is much easier initiate legal prosecution in the case when some kind of wrongdoing has been committed. Although even in such cases, political considerations may have an impact on such a decision. Consider a situation where representatives of the *ancien regime* enjoy significant popular support. In such a case, there may be opportunity for only the so-called limited criminal sanction, in other words "prosecution processes that do not necessarily culminate in full punishment".[2]

The second issue is whether the law has been changed in the course of the transition, questioning whether representatives of the *ancien regime* had acted legally when they committed deeds considered wrongdoings by the new regime. In such cases, the decision to start investigations against the *ancien regime* is always political, for there is a need to act retrospectively. Such cases pose a special dilemma in a political transition from autocracy to democracy: acting in the name of rule of law may paradoxically require actions that are contradictory to that principle. The case of border guards of the German Democratic Republic, who shot people trying to cross the Berlin wall is a well-known example. They were brought to trial despite the fact that they acted in accordance with the law at the time. This case is also an exemplification of another dilemma of criminal justice applied in the conditions of political transition – the "dilemma of state crimes but individual responsibility".[3] In other words, the question is, who is to be brought to justice when we deal with structural violence? Responsibility for the implementation of any official state policy is usually diffused. Whenever such a policy results in the harm of citizens, the question inevitably appears – at what level do officials bear the primary responsibility? To what extent are the representatives of so-called street-level bureaucracy responsible for their acts done in accordance with the policy formulated by political leader(s)? The answers to these questions are less obvious when we think about wrongdoings, that are less drastic than killings, but which, nevertheless cause a significant damage either to individuals or to whole social groups.

The answers to both dilemmas are inevitably political in their nature. While such problems may appear in the context of any political transition, the very

2 Ruti G. Teitel, *Transitional Justice*, (New York: Oxford University Press, 2000), 47.
3 Ibid., 34.

fact that an incoming regime becoming aware of these dilemmas is rather possible in the cases typical for transitions from a less to more liberal regime. Such awareness is possible when the scope of rights and freedoms guaranteed by the incoming regime is wider than under the *ancien regime*. Contemporary jurisprudence on criminal justice in the transitional context is based on the legacy of the Nuremberg trial precedent, which linked the accountability for state policies with international law regulating human rights.[4] Hence, inconsistency of the *ancien regime's* policies with international human rights norms help mitigate the basic dilemma of retrospective justice. The solution to the dilemma of individual responsibility, however, remains rather a matter of design for each particular transitional justice policy. Using international law as a basis for justification of transitional criminal prosecutions also means that there is a "natural" limitation in the application of amnesty (which is one of the possible outcomes of investigations and trials), which is defined by the so-called international crimes (crimes against humanity, genocide and war crimes).

The literature on transitional justice does not provide any clear theoretical framework to connect the implementation of investigations and trials in the context of political transition and political development. As a result, only general hypothetical expectations can be devised. According to Ruti Teitel's fundamental work, the main function of transitional criminal proceedings is to rebuild trust in the rule of law. In this approach, the role of criminal prosecutions "transcends that of conventional punishment";[5] they become one of the foundational acts of a new regime confirming its sovereignty (understood as the state's ability to control its territory and population). Of course, such an expectation would be legitimate only in the case when the incoming regime is committed to the principle of the rule of law. Taking into account the above considerations, one can assume that the impact of transitional criminal justice on political development depends not on the quantitative indicators characterizing it (e.g. the number of convicted officials, the average degree of penalty), but on how the abovementioned dilemmas are solved and whether the solution is regarded by the society as *legitimate* and perceived as *just*. If it is not achieved, no matter whether there are massive penalties or full amnesty, there is a risk that such policies could lead to political destabilisation.

In this context, the analysis of transitional justice proposed by Jon Elster deserves attention. Elster draws attention to the meaning of emotions as drivers

---

4 Ibid., 31–33.

5 Ibid., 66.

of transitional justice. In particular, he argues that the intensity of the so-called retributive emotions (anger, Cartesian indignation, hatred, contempt and Aristotelian indignation) as well as some specific cultural features of the society that prevent emotions to decay with the passage of time, shape the legal expressions of transitional justice.[6] Following this logic, we may expect that the scope of criminal prosecutions may greatly depend on the gravity of wrongdoings committed by the *ancien regime*. If a significant part of society is personally harmed by the actions of the government, one can expect a more intensive demand for bringing the representatives of the government to justice (in other words, a stricter policy of criminal prosecution will be perceived as just). Additionally, one can expect a larger demand when the memories of wrongdoings are fresh. These are intuitive expectations that can be regarded as hypotheses rather than proven facts.

The existing empirical research proves the signalled hypothetical expectations only partially. Countries with the highest levels of violence in the past prove more likely to grant amnesty without trials.[7] The same research signals another important constraint for applying trials as mechanisms of transitional justice – economic performance of the state. Investigations and trials are costly, so the decision to apply them may depend on whether there are enough financial resources.[8] The experience of the post-communist transitions in Central and Eastern European countries suggests that despite obvious large-scale abuses, trials have not become the most popular mechanism of transitional justice due to the complexity of answers to the abovementioned dilemmas in practical terms, but also due to the awareness among the political elites that large-scale punishment may lead to the creation of new cleavages and social costs; the final impact of which on politics is not always predictable. Nevertheless, the conclusions drawn from the comparison of such complicated issues as trials should not be taken for granted as predictors of how trials may look like in individual, yet unstudied cases. Undoubtedly, the analysis of criminal prosecutions as mechanisms of transitional justice as well as their impact on political development of a country should take into account the specific circumstances of the case under scrutiny.

---

6 Jon Elster, *Closing the Books. Transitional Justice in Historical Perspective*, (Cambridge: Cambridge University Press, 2004), 216–244.

7 Tricia D. Olsen, Leigh A. Payne, Andrew G. Reiter, *Transitional Justice in Balance. Comparing processes, weighing efficacy*, (Washington D.C.: United States Institute of Peace Press, 2010), 58.

8 Ibid., 77.

2.2. Scale of violence

The Euromaidan protests of 2013 and 2014 is certainly one of the most significant events in the history of independent Ukraine. There are many reasons for such a statement. Most importantly, is the unprecedented scale of violence that accompanied the protests. For the first time since 1991, a political conflict in Ukraine resulted in bloodshed. The first instance of using violence happened in the night of 29–30 November 2013, when *Berkut* special police forces were used against the initial small-scale protest, consisting of predominantly young people with a pro-European orientation. As a result of this event, between 60 and 91 people were injured and up to 10 were hospitalised.[9] The attempt to suppress the protest brought on the opposite effect and ultimately led to an escalation. The first deaths happened on 22 January 2014, when two protesters were killed by gunshots and two others received firearm injuries, later dying in hospital.[10] The culmination of the confrontation took place between 18 and 21 February 2014, when lethal weapons were massively used by the police, resulting in around 100 casualties,[11] mainly among protesters, but also among police officers.[12] These numbers reflect only the situation in Kyiv, the most significant stage of the protests but not the only one. At least eight people were reported to have been killed outside Kyiv.[13]

Along with the gravest instances of violence, other wrongdoings should also be taken into account. First and foremost was the limitation of political rights and freedoms, symbolized primarily by the so-called "dictatorial laws" adopted on 16 January 2014. These were accompanied by politically motivated prosecutions of protesters in which law enforcement and judiciary officials were involved. Secondly, the authorities provided support to affiliated criminal groups (so-called *titushki*[14]), who additionally acted against the Euromaidan protesters and activists and whose acts resulted in numerous injuries, kidnappings and destruction of

---

9 International Advisory Panel, 'Report of the International Advisory Panel on its review of the Maidan Investigations', 31 March 2015, 12.

10 Ibid., 17.

11 People killed during the final days of the protest are commonly referred to as the "heavenly hundred". The significance of this notion will be explained in chapter 4, devoted to historical justice.

12 International Advisory Panel, supra n 9, at 21.

13 The International Federation for Human Rights, 'The price of Freedom. Summary of the public report of human rights organizations on crimes against humanity committed during the period of Euromaidan', 23 February 2015, 6.

14 A term used to describe hooligans unofficially engaged by the authorities to support police forces in their actions against the opposition. *Titushki* were supposed to imitate

property. The exact number of such cases remains unknown and the precise scale of such relatively low-intensity violence that took place during the Euromaidan is yet to be uncovered.

The crucial feature of these wrongdoings is their systemic nature: "There is a clear connection between actions of paramilitary groups, the law enforcement, the Prosecutor's Office, the judiciary, decisions of the parliament and the government, and statements by high-level state officials".[15] Evidence supporting the thesis that the response to the Euromaidan protests and its further development was coordinated at the highest political level was found in the presidential residence of Mezhyhirya and later published by investigative journalist Sergii Leshchenko.[16] In other words, there is every reason to believe that the actions of Ukraine's authorities during the Euromaidan were far from legitimate, incompatible with the basic principles of a democratic state.

2.3. Demand for transitional investigations and trials

Whenever a political transition is accompanied with direct violence, calls for retaliation are usually strong and the transitional governments have to face them in order to maintain their legitimacy. The situation with Ukraine immediately following the end of the Euromaidan protests is no exception. In the evening of 21 February 2014, when the agreement between Viktor Yanukovych and the opposition leaders was reached and shootings in the centre of Kyiv stopped, the protesters remained in the central square of Kyiv in order to honour the memory of those who died during previous several days. In a dramatic speech announced by Volodymyr Parasyuk, one of the representatives of the Euromaidan Self-defence[17] who later became an MP, set a deadline for Yanukovych to resign by 10:00 am on 22 February and threatened to attack the presidential administration building if this requirement was not fulfilled.[18] The threat appeared to be unnecessary as Viktor Yanukovych had already escaped the capital that evening.

---

public dissatisfaction with opposition's activities. The name originated from a surname of one of such persons, who was recognized thanks to his account in the social media.

15 The International Federation for Human Rights, supra n 13 at 4.

16 Sergii Leshchenko, *Mezhyhirskyy syndrome. Diagnoz vladi Yanukovycha*, (Kyiv: Brayt Buks, 2014), 210–228.

17 A group of protesters that emerged after the first dispersal of Euromaidan aimed at protecting participants from police violence.

18 The recording of the speech is available on the Hromadske. TV channel: https://youtu.be/4ys0FDfXQak (accessed 12 February 2016).

As it became clear later, preparations of the former president to flee began long before the speech was delivered, hence Parasyuk's ultimatum was not the "moment that changed history" of Ukraine (as it was widely described in social media). Nevertheless, the speech itself, as well as the enthusiastic reaction to it from the public, contrasted significantly with the restrained reaction to the speeches of the opposition leaders who presented the achieved agreement with Yanukovych. It was exactly a moment in which the emotions of thousands of people, many of whom witnessed mass deaths just several hours prior, could easily be turned into an act of revenge. The issue of investigation and trials had, of course, not been discussed during that meeting, but the expectation that Viktor Yanukovych himself as well as representatives of his administration had to be brought to justice was clear.

Activists remained on the Independence Square (Maidan) through summer 2014. Immediately after the fall of the Yanukovych regime, the Euromaidan movement transformed itself into a kind of grassroots watchdog initiative. Although not being an institution able to represent the society as a whole in a legitimate way, it exerted significant pressure on the politicians. The members of parliament who took responsibility for the political situation in the country on 22 February 2014 certainly understood the gravity of the situation compounded by the readiness of the emotionally-loaded crowd to "take matters into their own hands" (one more popular saying at that time). On the same day, representatives of the Euromaidan formed the Circle of People's Trust, which defined itself as the "intermediary between the Maidan and managers, hired by people to conduct public service". On 26 February 2014, one day before Arseniy Yatsenyuk's interim government was formed, an unprecedented ceremony which presented to the Maidan proposals of new ministers for the interim government took place. Although it did not have any legal basis, the ceremony served as an additional tool to legitimise the interim government in the eyes of the public. In such circumstances, expectations of the activists, which included bringing the representatives of Yanukovych administration to justice, could not be ignored by politicians who took the stage after the Euromaidan.

The primary demand to judge the actions of Viktor Yanukovych and his entourage during the Euromaidan protests came from the protesters themselves. In other words, it was driven by a specific kind of a pressure group. The expectations towards a judicial response to Euromaidan-related violence of the whole society may be assessed as much more moderate. According to a survey conducted in December 2015, only 10.8 percent of respondents regarded the fact that the "Euromaidan killers are not punished" as an indicator of the "country's moving in the wrong direction".[19] Of course, this number does not prove that the issue of post-Euromaidan investigations is generally regarded as unimportant. It can be assumed that almost everyone would agree with the statements that good-quality investigation should be conducted.

The survey response, however, is important to assess the relative significance of the issue compared to other important political issues. From this perspective, the problem was overshadowed by other issues, such as the Donbas conflict[20] (72.6 percent), corruption (57 percent) and growing prices (68.9 percent). Another indicator of the society's low interest in investigations is the fact that court hearings regarding the Euromaidan-related cases, despite being open to the public, do not attract mass attention.[21] Hence, the most important question from the perspective of transitional justice is whether this issue is high on the list of priority problems for the society and thus whether the legal obligation to conduct good-quality investigations is combined with the political motivation of the authorities to create conditions necessary to do so. If the society does not regard the case as being important, one can hardly expect that even the best-quality investigation and trial would result in the perception of improvement in the field of rule of law.

2.4. Supply: policies addressing violence during the Euromaidan protests

The first days after the massacre in central Kyiv were marked by several decisions that had a significant impact on the discussed element of transitional justice in Ukraine. One of the first decisions taken by the *Verkhovna Rada* as early as 21 February 2014 was the announcement of unconditional amnesty for the Euromaidan protesters, as well as the annulment of several previous amnesties introduced during the protests (according to which the release of those arrested was conditioned by some form of concession from the protesters, therefore these amnesties were popularly called the "laws on hostages").[22] This answered some of the expectations of the protesters – further investigations and trials based on the

19 Source: Democratic Initiatives Foundation, http://dif.org.ua/ua/polls/2015a/2015-i-politichni-pidsumki---dumka-naselennja-.htm (accessed 11 March 2016).

20 This issue will be discussed in Chapter 5.

21 Yevgieniya Zakrievskaya, 'Obratnaya storona ochevidnosti', *Zerkalo Nedeli*, 18 December 2015.

22 Law of Ukraine, 'On avoidance of prosecution and punishment of persons because of events that occurred during peaceful gatherings, and annulment of some laws of Ukraine', no. 743-VII, adopted 21 February 2014.

assumption that it was the political elite who was responsible for the outbreak of the conflict. The challenge then was to translate the general belief that it is Yanukovych himself responsible for what happened into quality investigations and trials. First and foremost, this meant any punishment for those responsible for the violence should correspond with the principles of Ukraine's criminal law, which to a large extent is not different from the principles typical for a European democracy. In particular, Ukraine's criminal code contains the *nullum crimen sine lege* principle and also clearly prohibits the retrospective application of criminal accountability.[23] These principles are aimed exactly at protecting individuals from arbitrary use of criminal repressions. These may naturally contradict the public perception of what is just in a given situation. This subchapter is primarily aimed at exploring how a transitional approach to criminal accountability is used to solve this problem.

On 22 February 2014, the parliament reversed the 2010 judgement of the Constitutional Court of Ukraine (CCU),[24] and so *de facto* re-introduced a parliamentary regime. Of course, the very fact that the legislature issues a decree annulling the judgement of a constitutional court cannot be regarded as something ordinary and acceptable in the practice of European constitutionalism. What may justify this step is the fact that the 2010 judgement of the CCU itself was not faultless from the legal point of view. The Venice Commission, which examined the constitutional situation in Ukraine in 2010, has not criticised the movement as illegitimate, but pointed at problematic aspects of a situation created by the judgement, which raised "questions of the legitimacy of past actions, as the institutions of Ukraine worked for several years on the basis of constitutional rules later declared unconstitutional". Finally, it encouraged "the Ukrainian authorities to engage in a process of constitutional change based on the regular constitutional procedure for constitutional amendments and on the democratic participation of all actors of society concerned".[25] Having in mind the legacy of Yanukovych's presidency, one may more easily agree with the opinion that was rather dominant in the Ukrainian public debate in 2010, namely that the CCU was used as a political tool to widen the competencies of the then newly-elected president.

---

23 Law of Ukraine 'Criminal Code of Ukraine', no. 2341-III, adopted 5 April 2001.

24 Decree of the Verkhovna Rada of Ukraine, 'On the text of the Constitution of Ukraine in the wording of 28 June 1996, as amended and supplemented by the laws of Ukraine of 8 December 2003 no. 2222-IV, of 1 February 2011 no. 2952-VI, of 19 September 2013 no. 586-VII', no. 750-VII, adopted 22 February 2014.

25 European Commission for Democracy through Law, 'Opinion on the constitutional situation in Ukraine', no. CDL-AD(2010)044, 20 December 2010.

It is not the goal of this discussion to assess the legal and procedural accuracy of the 2010 judgement nor the 2014 decree – that is rather a task for lawyers. This analysis, however, is based on the assumption that in both cases, the decisions were driven by political motivation, and what is of interest for the purposes of this analysis is the political consequences of these decisions. In the cited decree of 22 February 2014, the parliament used the argumentation presented by the Venice Commission, stating that as a result of the CCU judgement, the president "enjoys far more powers than could be foreseen by the voters when he was elected". From the perspective of the discussed dimension of transitional justice in Ukraine, the significance of this decree is in the fact that it paved the way to treat the actions of the former president as a usurpation of power[26] and search for accountability for the whole period of his presidency, not only for the time between 21 November 2013 and 21 February 2014.

The decree annulling the judgement of the CCU was followed by the decree of the parliament that ascertained the fact that the judges of the CCU had broken their oath when issuing the judgement in 2010.[27] On the basis of that same document, the *Verkhovna Rada* dismissed five of the constitutional judges it appointed and urged the President and the Congress of Judges to do the same with the judges from their quota,[28] it also advised the Prosecutor General's Office of Ukraine (PGOU) to initiate a criminal investigation on the ill-fated 2010 judgement and "bring all those responsible to justice". Criminal investigations against the constitutional judges have indeed begun.

Surfing on the wave of intensive emotions following the bloodshed on Kyiv's Maidan, the parliament has undertaken an attempt to frame Euromaidan-related violence as a crime against humanity. On 25 February 2014, the *Verkhovna Rada* adopted a declaration on the acceptance of jurisdiction of the International Criminal Court (ICC) over the alleged crimes committed on its territory between

26 Actions aimed at seizing power are defined as a crime in article 109 of the Criminal Code of Ukraine.

27 Decree of the Verkhovna Rada of Ukraine, 'On reacting to facts of breaking the oath of judge by judges of the Constitutional Court of Ukraine', no. 775-VII, adopted 24 February 2014.

28 Judges of the Constitutional Court of Ukraine were elected (and could be recalled) by the President, the Parliament and the Congress of Judges of Ukraine (the highest self-governing body of the judiciary), with each appointing one third of the bench of 18 seats.

21 November 2013 and 22 February 2014.[29] On 17 April 2014, the government of Ukraine lodged a declaration under article 12(3) of the Rome Statute to the ICC.

Ukraine's relations with the ICC are quite complicated. In 2000, Ukraine signed the Rome Statute of the ICC, but due to the negative verdict of the CCU issued in 2001, the document has not been ratified. However, the CCU did not issue a fundamental objection to the principles of the Rome Statute; the obstacle indicated was rather a technical one. According to the Court, the Ukrainian constitution does not foresee the possibility to complement the national criminal jurisdiction.[30] Nevertheless, ratification could not happen without an appropriate amendment of the constitution. Hence, the debate on the ratification of the Rome Statute was frozen for over a decade due to the fact that Ukraine was neither a subject nor an object of acts covered by the jurisdiction of the ICC. Therefore in the eyes of Ukraine's political elite the problem had a theoretical nature. The reality forced the issue of cooperation with the ICC only to return on the agenda in the aftermath of the bloody culmination of the Euromaidan protests. It should be stressed that the adoption of the abovementioned declaration does not mean ratification by Ukraine of the Rome Statute but rather *ad hoc* acceptance of the exercise of jurisdiction of the ICC according to article 12(3) of the Statute.

An analysis of the debate in the *Verkhovna Rada* that preceded the vote for the declaration suggests that the main motivation of the MPs was to create an official document containing the list of those to be blamed for the recent violence. To a large extent, the debate turned into a bidding on whose names should be mentioned in the declaration. One of the typical statements went as following: "I appeal to you, dear colleagues, [let's include] without a debate: Yanukovych, Zakharchenko, Arbuzov, Klyuyev, Azarov, Pshonka, Lukash and so on. We include them and lodge the case to the court. And let the independent court examine their cases." In other words, the debate revealed a complete lack of understanding of international criminal justice among the MPs adopting the declaration. In their perception, the document was equal to an indictment lodged to an independent "Hague Tribunal" which would without any doubt result in the

29 Statement of the Verkhovna Rada of Ukraine to the International Criminal Court on recognition by Ukraine of jurisdiction of the International Criminal Court on crimes against humanity committed by top state officials, which have led to serious consequences, and mass murder of Ukrainian citizens during peaceful protests in the period from 21 November 2013 to 22 February 2014, no. 790-VII, adopted 25 February 2014.

30 The full text of the verdict of the Constitutional Court of Ukraine is available in the online database of Ukrainian legislation: http://zakon1.rada.gov.ua/laws/show/v003v710-01.

conviction of the ones listed. Only several voices during the debate revealed an understanding of the principles of independence of the ICC's investigations (that is, the course of investigation can by no means be influenced by the fact of mentioning any names in the declaration on acceptance of the ICC jurisdiction).[31] As a result, the version of the declaration adopted by the parliament alleges the direct responsibility of Viktor Yanukovych, his prosecutor-general Viktor Pshonka and interior minister Vitaliy Zakharchenko (along with "other officials who gave and executed clearly criminal orders and who can be identified by the prosecutor of the International Criminal Court"). It was a completely unnecessary step dictated exclusively by the political motivation of politicians to show that they supported a document that may serve as an additional proof of their personal accusation of the alleged author of Euromaidan-related violence.

This attempt to use the declaration of acceptance of the ICC jurisdiction as a political step to meet public expectations still driven by extremely vivid emotions of mass killings that took place just four days earlier and additionally to internationalize the case by underlining that the gravity of alleged crimes of the former president and his entourage was eventually abolished by the ICC itself. In November 2015, the ICC's Office of the Prosecutor stated that the repressions against the Euromaidan "were rather a reaction to events [...] and aimed to limit the protests rather than being part of a deliberate, coordinated plan of violence methodologically carried out against the protest movement".[32] In other words, the ICC rejected the MPs' argumentation that there were crimes against humanity.

This decision, however, did not end Ukraine's attempts to engage the ICC into its transitional justice efforts. In September 2015, the Ukrainian government lodged a second *ad hoc* acceptance of the ICC jurisdiction according to article 12(3) of the Rome Statute. This one refers to the armed conflict in Donbas, an issue that will be discussed in chapter 5. Nevertheless, when it comes to post-Euromaidan criminal justice, the Ukrainian authorities remained on their own with the responsibility for quality of ongoing investigations.

The *Berkut* special police units became one of first objects of criminal prosecution in the aftermath of the Maidan killings. One of the first decisions of the new interim minister of interior Arsen Avakov was about disbanding the *Berkut* units, which happened on 25 February 2014. The heads of the ministry's regional branches were to decide about the professional future of around 4,000 members

31 The transcript was retrieved from the official website of the Verkhovna Rada of Ukraine: http://rada.gov.ua/meeting/stenogr.

32 International Criminal Court. The Office of the Prosecutor, 'Report on Preliminary Examination Activities (2015)', 12 November 2015.

of staff serving in the units. Internal investigations on the behaviour of the officers had to be conducted within the fifteen days that followed.[33] Such a quick reaction was undoubtedly driven by public outrage targeted at the *Berkut*. It led to the escape of many *Berkut* officers to Russia (and also to annexed Crimea), where they were praised as heroes, granted Russian citizenship and joined the Russian security forces.

It took, however, much more time to institutionalize this element of transitional justice. On 18 December 2014, ten months after the bloody culmination of the Euromaidan protests, a unit for special investigations was created within the structure of the PGOU with the task to coordinate all inquiries on the "usurpation of power and the whole complex of criminal activities committed during the period of Viktor Yanukovych's presidency".[34] According to Sergiy Horbatyuk, the head of the unit and deputy Prosecutor General of Ukraine, the investigation of Euromaidan-related violence considers the following course of events. First, Viktor Yanukovych and his entourage committed acts aimed at the usurpation of power. In this context, the mentioned examination of some decisions of the CCU is taking place. Second, within the same period of time, Yanukovych and his entourage committed a number of economic crimes. Finally, when protests started, a decision was taken to disperse demonstrations, oppress the activists and eventually kill the protesters. According to the PGOU, the order to disperse demonstrations was given by Yanukovych personally. The most important issue is that "the main motive of cruelty of Yanukovych's surrounding was the desire to continue plundering the country and the fear of losing power, because they knew that they would be held responsible for what they had done".[35] This version was publicly confirmed by Viktor Shokin, the Prosecutor General of Ukraine (February 2015–March 2016), who stated in a much more straightforward manner that the case has in fact been explained: the crimes against the Euromaidan have

33 Web portal of Ukrainian Government, 'Arsen Avakov pidpysav nakaz pro likvidatsiyu spetspidrozdilu "Berkut"', http://www.kmu.gov.ua/control/uk/publish/article?art_id=247057542&cat_id=244276429 (accessed 10 March 2016).

34 Website of the Prosecutor General's Office of Ukraine, 'Upravlinnya spetsialnyh rozsliduvan Henprokuratury ocholyv Serhiy Horbatyuk – prokuror z 20-ty richnym stazhem slidchoyi diyalnosti', http://www.gp.gov.ua/ua/news.html?_m=publications&_c=view&_t=rec&id=148237 (accessed 10 March 2016).

35 Pavel Sheremet, Sevgil Musayeva-Borovyk, 'Serhiy Horbatyuk: My blyzki do zavershennya spravy Mezhyhirya', *Ukrayinska Pravda*, 19 February 2016.

been performed by a criminal group headed by former president Yanukovych.[36] In other words, the official understanding of events goes more or less in line with what can be called "a common knowledge about the most recent history of Ukraine", at least as it is seen from the perspective of that part of Ukrainian society who supported the ideas of the Euromaidan: The wrongdoings described should be regarded as a consequence of previous crimes of predominantly economic nature, a violent element of the specific cascade of criminal activity that was grounded in the very political system of the state.

At the moment of writing the book, two years after the events that triggered the discussed investigation, the version of events proposed by the state prosecution has not been confirmed by the relevant decision of the court. At the same time, as it was mentioned earlier, investigations continue to take place. In November 2015, on the second anniversary of the outbreak of Euromaidan, the PGOU reported about 281 notifications of suspicions, 123 indictments lodged in the courts and 28 court decisions. Among economic crimes committed by the state's highest officials, the PGOU mentions large-scale embezzlement of public funds and property, tax evasion and smuggling, bribery, money laundering and using fiscal and law-enforcement agencies to eliminate competition and appropriate their private property and capital shares.[37]

Generally, the existing court decisions refer to direct perpetrators of violence (police officers and *titushki*); in the case of the highest officials, including Viktor Yanukovych himself, the PGOU is unable to move further than a suspicion of committing criminal offence. This may be explained by the fact that the suspects are beyond the borders of Ukraine, mainly in Russia, which does not express the will to cooperate with Ukrainian law-enforcement agencies, including through international structures like Interpol, thus providing *de facto* political asylum for Viktor Yanukovych and his closest colleagues. As a result, pre-trial investigation in these cases is conducted in accordance with a special procedure allowing the suspected to be convicted *in absentia*.

Investigations of Euromaidan-related cases has been an object of international scrutiny, both by NGOs as well as international organisations. One of the most

36 Irina Desyatnikova, Irina Kotsina, Aleksandr Shvets, 'Viktor Shokin: K sozhaleniyu, u mnogih nashih sotrudnikov, kak ya govoryu, v glazah tolko dollary', *Fakty*, 17 October 2015.

37 Website of the Prosecutor General's Office of Ukraine, 'Zlochyny proty Maydanu: rezultaty rozsliduvannya', http://www.gp.gov.ua/ua/news.html?_m=publications&_c=view&_t=rec&id=165726 (accessed 11 November 2015).

thorough assessments was conducted by the International Advisory Panel (IAP)[38] and published on 31 March 2015. The IAP report stressed such problems as lack of practical independence in circumstances where the investigating body belonged to the same authority as those under investigation; an absence of continuity at senior prosecutor level (caused by frequent changes of the prosecutor general); insufficient cooperation between the PGOU on the one hand and the ministry of interior and the Security Service of Ukraine on the other hand; court decisions that weaken the deterrent effect of the judiciary system (the IAP has noted, among others, the case of *Berkut* ex-commander Dmytro Sadovnyk, who had been notified of suspicion of 39 murders, but nevertheless released by court from pre-trial detention, which allowed him to escape the country).[39]

2.5. Effects and challenges

The first obvious conclusion from the above discussion is that the results of post-Euromaidan investigations two years after the end of the protests remain moderate in both quantitative and qualitative terms. The investigations focused on two types of wrongdoers: the direct executioners of the violence (the *Berkut* officers and *titushki*) and the highest officials, including Yanukovych, who allegedly created the predispositions for that violence. The overall picture of the organisational mechanisms that connect economic crimes at the top with unlawful use of force by the law enforcement agencies and mercenaries is yet to be proven in court (although it is widely discussed by investigative journalists).

The application of investigations and crimes as mechanisms of transitional justice in the Ukrainian case takes place in relatively comfortable circumstances. The post-Euromaidan political transition is characterised by a significant level of continuity, especially when it comes to legislation; thus, investigations and trials of wrongdoings committed under the presidency of Viktor Yanukovych do not face the problem of retroactivity. What may be seen as a problem is the nature of wrongdoings, especially the ones committed by the highest state officials. This means dealing with structural violence that is to be addressed by criminal justice. In other words, while there is no need to look for justification of criminal

38 An organ established by the Secretary General of the Council of Europe in order to oversee whether the investigations of incidents which took place in Ukraine from 30 November 2013 onwards met all the requirements of the European Convention on Human Rights and the case law of the European Court of Human Rights.

39 International Advisory Panel, supra n 9.

prosecutions against the representatives of the *ancien regime* that would explain how they fit into the principle of the rule of law, there is a challenge of bringing the right people to justice – the ones who are genuinely responsible for the wrongdoings of the regime.

Along with the mentioned challenge of general nature, the available information about the quality of investigations suggests the existence of several very specific challenges. First, Ukraine's law enforcement system and judiciary are technically outdated and inefficient. Second, there is undoubtedly an internal resistance within the law enforcement system and the judiciary, which were directly involved in repressions during the Euromaidan protests. For example, at the beginning of 2016, Sergiy Horbatyuk has publicly stated that there is a pressure exerted on the unit for special investigations from within the PGOU itself, aiming at influencing the course of the discussed post-Euromaidan investigations.[40]

The 281 notifications of suspicions that have a relation with the investigations obviously do not cover every person directly or indirectly involved in building the specific version of "oligarchic democracy" during the presidency of Viktor Yanukovych, or benefiting from it. One should also remember, that what can be called the specific "Yanukovych regime" was not a phenomenon isolated from the rest of Ukraine's political and economic system after 1991; it was a product of it.[41] Therefore, the hypothetical (at the moment of writing the book) conviction in all these cases would be important for a definite condemnation of the Yanukovych regime as an extreme deviation of the "oligarchic democracy", but it will not be a condemnation of that specific system in general, despite the fact that the mentioned Yanukovych's systemic violence was only possible in the framework of the "oligarchic democracy". Neither will it remove from the state apparatus the bearers of values specific for that regime. If we add the issue of post-Euromaidan investigations as not being ranked high on the list of society's expectations regarding how the state should start moving "in the right direction" (as pointed out

40 Public statement of Sergiy Horbatyuk in "Shuster LIVE" TV show, 22 April 2016, available online: https://youtu.be/0v3raANsT9k.

41 For example, Yanukovych started accumulating real estate that later became the well-known Mezhyhirya residence during Yushchenko's presidency and under support of the latter (Leshchenko, supra n 16 at 91–95). This fact should not be regarded as a kind of "proof" of Yushchenko's complicity in Yanukovych's later wrongdoings; it is just one more piece of evidence of the corrupted essence of Ukraine's political system allowing officials to use their positions for personal benefits and providing benefits to others, in the hope of later "repayment".

earlier), one cannot expect that the post-Euromaidan investigations and trials are sufficient tools to rebuild social trust in state institutions.

Rebuilding trust in the state in times of political flux requires additional efforts. Among them is a policy of vetting – a novelty that was introduced after the Euromaidan. The next chapter is specifically devoted to this practice.

3. Vetting

3.1. Theoretical background

Any transition between political regimes is a mixture of change and continuity. In particular, one should expect that in the aftermath of transition there will always be a part of society that represents values upon which the *ancien regime* was based. This problem may constitute a dilemma for the newly established regime claiming to respect the basic principles of democracy. On the one hand, equal rights is fundamental for democracy; yet on the other hand, there is a risk that the bearers of the abandoned values can "infect" the newly established democratic regime by introducing informal patterns of behaviour that do not correspond with the principles of democracy and the rule of law. All post-communist countries faced this dilemma in the early 1990s and most of them answered it by introducing vetting policies, also known as lustration.

Generally, lustration can be defined as an official policy aimed at revealing the truth about collaboration with or a position in the institutions of the *ancien regime* among certain categories of public officials and/or the ones applying for office under the new regime. An affirmative outcome of lustration usually results in the loss of position and/or limitation in access to public office for the screened individual. The scope of lustration policies may be different. Cynthia M. Horne proposes one of the clearest classifications that helps understand the diversity of lustration policies: (1) a wide and compulsory institutional change that resulted in expansive and obligatory purge of public bureaucracy (such as in Estonia, Latvia and Czech Republic); (2) a narrow and voluntary institutional change that is based on the public disclosure of appropriate facts and limited purge of officials (as was in Poland, Hungary and Lithuania); (3) a symbolic change that is based only on public disclosure of facts about the past (Romania, Bulgaria, Slovakia); and (4) no lustration – this can be seen in Ukraine prior to 2014, as well as in Russia.[1]

The design of lustration policies can be interpreted as the introduction of collective responsibility – whether an individual falls under the requirement to be screened depends on his or her belonging to a certain category of citizens. According to Ruti Teitel, "civil sanctions of an administrative nature are based on exclusionary conditions, chiefly of political loyalty, systematically disqualifying

1 Cynthia M. Horne, 'The Impact of Lustration on Democratization in Postcommunist Countries', *The international Journal of Transitional Justice*, vol. 8 (2014): 508–510.

entire classes from participation in the new government".[2] Without a doubt such a "loose read" of the rule of law principle can be acceptable only in extraordinary conditions of a transitional period. The justification for it is based on the fact that "the tyranny of the modern bureaucratic state diffuses responsibility through polity".[3] Specific questions that arise here include: To which extent loyalty to a previous regime should be regarded as dangerous? How to define symptoms of that loyalty? How to assess the willingness of an individual to switch his or her loyalty to a new regime? And finally, whether it is enough only to "reveal the truth" about one's past or should the fact of being a part of the *ancient regime* automatically exclude an individual from the possibility to continue civil service? The answers to these questions define the specific designs of lustration policies and they are essentially political. As a result, there is no case of lustration policy that has not faced criticism of being incompatible with the basic principles of democracy (as we will see further, Ukraine is no exception). Due to this fact, countries implementing lustration policies usually faced the wave of appellations from the ones affected by the policies and thus developed a significant jurisprudence in this field. In Europe, steps have been made to create a set of standard basic norms regulating the practice of lustration, which took the form of a resolution of the Parliamentary Assembly of the Council of Europe (CoE), adopted in 1996. The resolution contains guidelines for the countries willing to implement lustration in order to ensure that they comply with the principles of the rule of law. The document notes that any lustration policy should ensure that responsibility under lustration laws be applied individually, that the right to a defence and the presumption of innocence until proven guilty should be guaranteed. Finally, the resolution states that "the aim of lustration is not to punish people presumed guilty – this is the task of prosecutors using criminal law – but to protect the newly emerging democracy".[4] The existence of such guidelines do not deny the fact that the very decision to implement a vetting policy, as well as the scope of it, remains in the domain of politics. The guidelines are nothing more than an attempt to assure that a move away from the rule of law is constrained by some predictable rules, as long as it is motivated by a desire to strengthen democracy.

From a theoretical point of view, lustration refers to one central problem of political science, namely the considerations to which extent institutions matter

---

2 Ruti G. Teitel, *Transitional Justice*, (New York: Oxford University Press, 2000), 150.

3 Ibid.

4 Resolution of the Parliamentary Assembly of the Council of Europe, 'Measures to dismantle the heritage of former communist totalitarian systems', no. 1096 (1996), adopted 27 June 1996.

in shaping the behaviour of citizens. Most students of contemporary democracy would agree that they do, but at the same time there is also a consensus that institutions are strongly influenced by the environment in which they emerge and develop.[5] In other words, lustration constitutes an attempt of a newly established political regime to modify conditions under which institutions of this regime consolidate. While it is relatively easy to change formal rules, dealing with informal ones might take much more time and effort. The ultimate goal is to eliminate the "bad social capital",[6] where "bad" is undoubtedly defined as contrary to the fundamental values of the newly established political regime. From this perspective, lustration can be regarded as essentially a forward-oriented policy which, in turn, creates doubts as to whether it can be treated as an element of transitional justice.

One can say that vetting policies generally address the same problems as transitional criminal justice. As it has been stressed in chapter 2, finding a proper balance between individual responsibility of highest state officials and lowest-level executive officials constitutes one of principal challenges of criminal justice in the context of political transition. Vetting can be regarded as a supplementary policy that may help the newly established regime to answer this challenge: while criminal justice brings punishment to the ones who are personally responsible for the most significant wrongdoings of the *ancien regime*, lustration is introduced as a preventive measure to hedge the incoming regime from the ones whose personal responsibility is not evident, but highly probable. Whenever both policies are applied in the conditions of transition from a less to more liberal political regime, they are constrained by a similar paradox of the need to act in conflict with the principle of the rule of law in order to strengthen the perception that the rule of law is actually reinforced. The key difference between transitional criminal justice and vetting is that the former is supposed to have an "automatic" nature (if there is a crime, there should be punishment), the latter has essentially an arbitrary nature. In other words, vetting is always a political act. Thus, it is much more dependent on a political demand and supply than investigations and trials.

Finally, it is important to ask how effective lustration policies are and consequently what may be the expected political outcome of lustration policy in the case of Ukraine. There seems to be a consensus that lustration in Central and Eastern European states had a positive impact on consolidating democracy. According to Cynthia M. Horne, lustration is associated with higher final levels

5 Adam Przeworski, 'Institutions Mater?', *Government and Opposition*, vol. 39, no. 4 (2004); 527–540.

6 Natalia Letki, 'Lustration and Democratisation in East-Central Europe', *Europe-Asia Studies*, Vol. 54, No. 4 (2002): 540.

of democracy; furthermore, "more compulsory or punitive programs evidence relationships of significantly larger magnitude to overall democratization than programs relying on more voluntary means of bureaucratic change".[7] Natalia Letki generally confirms the positive impact of lustration on democratization, but distances herself from the statement that there is a strong causal relationship. According to Letki, "a successful introduction of screening can be considered analogous to Przeworski's threshold of economic development: a country which successfully puts a lustration law into force marks its break with the past".[8] Both cited works are based on comparative analysis of lustration policies implemented in post-communist countries. A more nuanced case study of Polish lustration does not deny the positive effects, but emphasizes that it has also negative consequences, in particular the use of lustration as a tool to discredit political opponents.[9] As in the case of criminal justice, one can expect that the impact of vetting policies on the political development of the state should be analysed in the context of its specific political circumstances. As we will see below, vetting policies in post-Euromaidan Ukraine differ significantly from other well-studied cases of post-communist lustrations. It is much more oriented primarily towards the post-1991 period; the transition that preceded the introduction of the policy is characterized by a significant level of continuity. In other words, it is more difficult to distinguish what belongs to the "bad" past. As a result, there is a challenge in clearly defining the "undesirable" categories of public officials. This, in turn, means that one can expect a much more politicized process of lustration than in the cases when the difference between political regimes is more obvious.

3.2. Demand for vetting

A "reboot of authorities"[10] became one of the most popular slogans during the Euromaidan protests in Ukraine. The desire to change authorities was one of the principal motivations of the protesters physically present in the revolutionary camp in

7 Horne, supra n 1 at 514.

8 Letki, supra n 6 at 548.

9 Marta Zięba, 'To what extent is lustration an effective mechanism of transitional justice and democratic consolidation? The case of Poland', *Security and Human Rights*, no. 2 (2012): 157–158.

10 Ukr.: *перезавантаження влади.*

the centre of Kyiv in February 2014.[11] Importantly, this demand to "reboot authorities" should be understood primarily as a demand to replace the governing elite, which proved to be unaccountable and responsible for the disappointing quality of life in the country. This demand, however, did not refer to the institutional design of the political system as such, but to the mentioned "bad social capital" that dominated most public institutions. As a result, the primary demand for vetting policies was qualitatively different than the one which drove vetting policies in Central European states. In the Ukrainian case, it was the political elites responsible for the political and economic situation in the country post-1991, under the "oligarchic democracy", that eventually culminated in the notorious protest.

There are no systematic data available that would allow for an assessment as to whether there was a demand for post-communist lustration in Ukraine immediately after 1991 and how it evolved in subsequent years. Yet, what is clear is that the issue of lustration was virtually absent from Ukrainian public discourse in the 1990s. The problem was raised sporadically by former dissidents and intellectuals,[12] but never became a major political issue. Public opinion was focused on everyday socio-economic problems which, however, remained unsolved as time passed. The wave of protests during the Orange Revolution of 2004 also did not raise the issue of "rebooting the authorities" to the category of a major political issues. A survey conducted before the repeated second round of presidential elections in 2004 revealed that in the case of repeated falsification, a relative majority of Ukrainians (31.5 percent) was convinced that everyone should accept the outcome in order to maintain stability and peace; only 25.5 percent of respondents believed that such falsification should be questioned in court.[13] In other words, Ukrainians were predominantly ready to accept peace at the price of justice. In 2014, the violent confrontation between the authorities and a significant part of society radicalised expectations of the latter.

Like in the case of the demand for the criminal prosecution of Viktor Yanukovych and his entourage, the primary demand for lustration originated from the Euromaidan activists in the atmosphere of uncertainty that followed the first days after the massacre in the centre of Kyiv. The already mentioned Circle of People's

---

11 According to surveys conducted during the protest by the Democratic Initiatives Foundation, http://www.dif.org.ua/ua/polls/2014_polls/vid-maidanu-taboru-do-maidan.htm (accessed 20 March 2016).

12 For example: Mykola Ryabchuk, *Ulyublenyy pistolet pani Simpson. Hronika pomaranchevoyi porazky*, (K.I.S.: Kyiv, 2009), 74–77.

13 'Hromadyanska reaktsiya na falsyfikatsiyu rezultativ vyboriv i politychnu kryzu', *Natsionalna bezpeka i oborona*, no. 10 (2004): 13.

Trust formulated expectations towards the members of the interim government. Key among them was not having close relations with the administration of Viktor Yanukovych and Mykola Azarov's cabinet of ministers as well as not being on the list of the 100 richest Ukrainians.[14] This represented the first attempt to formulate vetting criteria by banning access to government to those associated with the poor state of affairs in the country. On 26 February 2014, during the public presentation of the interim government on the Maidan, the idea of establishing a lustration committee as an official state institution was expressed. Although this concept never materialized, it inspired a significant number of activists who, since that time, became the main proponents of the idea of lustration as a mechanism of post-Euromaidan transitional justice. Most of them have organised themselves into an NGO called the Civic Lustration Committee (Ukr. *Громадський Люстраційний Комітет*) which eventually became the strongest advocate of the idea of lustration in post-Euromaidan Ukraine. Yegor Sobolev, the head of the Committee, was elected to the *Verkhovna Rada* in October 2015, thus becoming one of the main promotors of the idea in parliament.

The idea of lustration was widely accepted and greeted by activists and civil society organisations. As illustrated in the following part of the chapter, it took nearly half a year for the parliament to adopt the law introducing lustration. In the meantime, the activists, mostly representing right-wing groups, started a practice of dumping allies of Viktor Yanukovych into garbage containers, a practice that became known as "street" or "garbage lustration".[15] Of course, such actions are contrary to the original idea of lustration. Nevertheless, the spreading popularity of this practice, as well as the growing popularity of the very notion of lustration, became an important indicator of a rising demand for a vetting policy especially among the most radicalized groups. From this perspective, lustration has become a kind of substitute for investigations and trials in the perception of the most active defenders of Euromaidan ideals. As seen in the previous chapter, investigations and trials are slow by nature, they are additionally hampered by the specificity of Ukraine's judiciary and law enforcement system. At the same time, lustration, although not being an act of revenge from a theoretical point of view, provides an immediate and visible effect that may be perceived as an act of justice.

At the same time, despite the growing popularity of the notion of lustration, there is no evidence that the demand for it was high in the scale of the whole

14 'Maydan oholosyv svoyi vymohy do maybutnih chleniv uryadu narodnoyi doviry', *Tyzhden*, 25 February 2014, http://tyzhden.ua/News/103135 (accessed 16 March 2016).

15 Tetiana Kozak, 'Good Riddance to Bad Rubbish?', *Transitions Online*, 20 October 2014.

society, beyond the radical groups of activists. On the one hand, the public awareness of existence of the policy is quite high. In October 2014, one month after the adoption of the law on lustration, 81.3 percent of Ukrainians admitted that they have heard about the law. Yet, when it comes to awareness of the essence of the policy – only 6 percent of the respondents admitted that they were well familiar with the provisions of the law; 49.7 percent stated that they know the provisions partially; while the rest admitted that they either do not know the provisions (41.4 percent) or that it is difficult to answer the question (2.9 percent). Also, the public opinion was far from being convinced that the law would lead to an improvement of the situation in Ukraine – only 14.8 percent of respondents were completely sure and 39.6 percent were rather sure that the law would have such an effect.[16] Figure 1 below presents an additional aspect of public perception of lustration – institutions, where the policy should be implemented first and foremost. What should be noted is the priority given to the parliament, an institution that, as we will see further, has been excluded from lustration.

Figure 1: Public perception of priority of institutions to be lustrated (October 2014)

Source: Razumkov Centre, http://www.razumkov.org.ua/ukr/poll.php?poll_id=993 (accessed 20 March 2016).

16 Source: Razumkov Centre, http://www.razumkov.org.ua/ukr/poll.php?poll_id=990; http://www.razumkov.org.ua/ukr/poll.php?poll_id=991; http://www.razumkov.org.ua/ukr/poll.php?poll_id=992 (accessed 20 March 2016).

According to a survey conducted in December 2014, only 21.2 percent of respondents regarded lustration as a priority.[17] One year later, the significance of lustration in the eyes of the public diminished – in December 2015, not more than 14.6 percent of respondents have identified lustration as an important indicator suggesting that the country was moving in the right direction (it is important to stress, however, that questions were formulated in a different way, so the cited numbers are not directly comparable and should be regarded as general indicators). Similar to the post-Euromaidan investigations, the issue of lustration is overshadowed by such problems as the war in Donbas, economic growth and – what is very important for the further analysis – fighting corruption.[18] This result may be interpreted as such: despite the fact that the idea of lustration is widely discussed in the media, it remains quite an abstract notion for most Ukrainians; at the same time, it should not be interpreted as a lack of expectations that the officials responsible for the state of affairs in the country be brought to justice.

As was mentioned earlier, the acts that can be regarded as wrongdoings by the majority of Ukrainians refer to the unsatisfactory quality of life. In other words, it is associated with the imminent problem of "monumental corruption"[19] that is a concrete and very specific thing that almost every Ukrainian has faced in his or her everyday experience. When having a choice between the abstract idea of lustration and the concrete idea of bringing corrupt officials to justice, there is a natural tendency to choose the latter. The awareness of existing corruption as well as its danger transcends all stages of political development of Ukraine since 1991, which is reflected in a number of surveys and reports dealing with the problem of corruption. In other words, corruption is the most significant problem that is expected to be eliminated from public life through the means of replacing the existing political elite, and support for it should be regarded as an additional indicator of support for the idea of lustration. The scale of the problem of corruption as seen by the Ukrainian public opinion on the eve of the Euromaidan events (October 2013) is presented in figure 2. As seen further, the design of Ukrainian lustration has taken this problem into account.

---

17 Source: Democratic Initiatives Foundation, http://dif.org.ua/ua/polls/2014_polls/jjorjojkpkhpkp.htm (accessed 20 March 2016).

18 Source: Democratic Initiatives Foundation, http://dif.org.ua/ua/polls/2015a/2015-i-politichni-pidsumki---dumka-naselennja-.htm (accessed 20 March 2016).

19 'Ukraine's Unyielding Corruption', *New York Times*, 31 March 2016.

Figure 2: Perception of corruption by Ukrainian public opinion (October 2013)

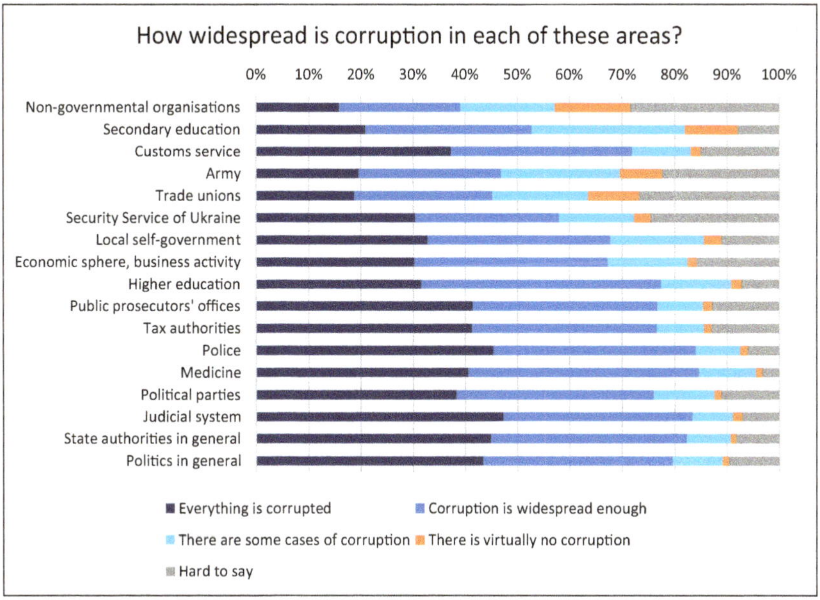

Source: Razumkov Centre, http://www.razumkov.org.ua/ukr/poll.php?poll_id=903 (accessed 20 March 2016).

In sum, the demand for vetting policies in post-Euromaidan Ukraine is an element of wider expectations to not only deal with the legacy of Viktor Yanukovych's presidency, but with the most significant problems of the whole post-1991 period. This particularly refers to the problem of corruption. When speaking about the society as a whole (putting aside the expectations of a narrow group of activists), it will be appropriate to claim that the demand for vetting is in essence a demand to deal with this particular problem, rather than an expectation to "punish" particular personalities as is the case of the demand for post-Euromaidan criminal justice.

3.3. Supply: design of vetting policies

The first proposals to introduce lustration in Ukraine appeared already at the beginning of 2005, soon after the Orange Revolution. Three draft laws were registered in the *Verkhovna Rada*. The first was submitted by MPs Vasyl Chervoniy and Serhiy Oleksiyuk of presidential block of parties called "Our Ukraine" and

Andriy Shkil from the Block of Yulia Tymoshenko (BYuT).[20] The second was proposed by Levko Lukyanenko, a well-known dissident representing BYuT.[21] The third came from Oleh Tyahnybok, the leader of the nationalist *Svoboda* party.[22] Due to the lack of a demand for lustration at that time, none of the drafts were voted on nor were they subject of public debate. What all three documents had in common was that the authors have strong anti-communist positions. As a result, the proposed visions of vetting policies at that time were addressed primarily at the legacy of the already-distant Soviet past, banning access of public office to officials of the Communist Party of the Soviet Union as well as KGB agents and collaborators. In other words, had the lustration policy been implemented after the Orange Revolution, it would have fit the pattern of "post-transitional justice" known from the Baltic states.[23] The only departure from that general pattern was foreseen by the first draft (by Chervoniy, Oleksiyuk and Shkil), which proposed to introduce a ban for persons involved in the falsification of the results of the 2004 presidential election – a delicate foretaste of the design for the vetting policy introduced one decade later. In the aftermath of the Euromaidan, the designers of the vetting policy had to take into account that it would not focus on the Soviet past as a primary concern.

The first element of the latest vetting policy in Ukraine is targeted at the judiciary. On 8 April 2014, a law "On the restoration of trust in the judicial power in Ukraine" was adopted.[24] As was highlighted in the explanatory note accompanying the draft law, the "defiantly unjust court decisions" during the Euromaidan protests have significantly hampered the public's trust in Ukraine's judicial system. This statement obviously corresponded with the reality – as it was mentioned above, around 80 percent of Ukrainians were convinced that the courts were corrupted, a fact that contradicts the possibility of the existence of trust in a public institution. The Euromaidan-related state-orchestrated violence obviously did not improve the situation. Therefore, an attempt to "eliminate dependence and corruption from the judicial system of Ukraine" was a logical first step. The law was intended to guarantee both high quality of trials against the highest officials of the

20 Draft law 'On lustration', no. 7028, registered 01 February 2005.

21 Draft law 'On certain restrictions on access to positions in the institutions of state authority of Ukraine', no. 7028-1, registered 04 February 2005.

22 Draft law 'On lustration', no. 7028-2, registered 02 March 2005.

23 Eva-Clarita Pettai, Vello Pettai, *Transitional and Retrospective Justice in the Baltic States*, (Cambridge: Cambridge University Press, 2015), 30.

24 Law of Ukraine 'On a restoration of trust in the judicial power in Ukraine', no. 1188-VII, adopted 08 April 2014.

Yanukovych regime and a just implementation of wider lustration in correspondence with the Council of Europe guidelines.

The law established a Special Temporary Commission of 15 members appointed by the Supreme Court, the *Verkhovna Rada* and a government representative for anti-corruption issues (a newly established position). The main task of the Commission is to screen the decisions of individual judges in order to determine whether they have broken their oaths by issuing unlawful decisions after 21 November 2013, which became *de facto* tools of repressions during the Euromaidan protests; by issuing decisions that limited the electoral rights of the opposition candidates during parliamentary elections in 2012 or by issuing decisions that were later undermined by the European Court of Human Rights. When the Commission concludes that a judge has broken his oath, the case is transferred to the High Council of Justice – a constitutional body that has a right to recommend the dismissal of a judge, which then should be accepted by the organ that appointed him or her (president or parliament). The Commission has been given a year to accomplish this tasks. Such a specific indirect mechanism of lustration has been introduced due to the fact that procedures of both approval and dismissal of judges are precisely defined in the constitution. Additionally, as a means to hedge the process from potential difficulties of a procedural nature, the transitional provisions of the law further terminated the mandates of all chairs and deputy chairs of courts across the country (importantly, this provision refers only to administrative functions, it does not deprive the affected persons from the status of judges). At the same time, the law also dismissed all current members of the self-governing and disciplinary bodies of the judiciary, the High Council of Justice (except *ex officio* members) and the High Qualification Commission for Judges, without the right to be re-appointed or re-elected.

Unlike the above-discussed law on the lustration of judges (as it is popularly called in Ukraine), it took much more time to design and adopt a major law on lustration. The first draft law was proposed by the *Svoboda* party on 26 March 2014.[25] The bill defined the main goal of lustration as a restoration of society's trust in public institutions. Importantly, the draft law has explicitly underlined the extraordinary nature of the act of lustration: According to the logic of the proposed law, other laws that regulate the status of affected persons can be applied only if they do not deny the law on lustration. The draft law has also indicated the categories of persons falling under lustration becoming a reference point for a further discussion on that issue. Along with former Soviet officials, the draft

25 Draft law 'On carrying out lustration in Ukraine', no. 4570, registered 26 March 2014.

included a detailed description of the officials of Yanukovych regime who should be banned from participating in public life. Additionally, the lustration measures were to be applied against the ones publicly undermining the state sovereignty of Ukraine. The bill also mentioned, although in a quite vague manner what later was called a "property lustration", a ban for officials unable to explain the source of their wealth. According to the draft law, the procedure was declaration-based. The ban was set up for a period of twenty years and criminal responsibility was foreseen for the obstruction of the lustration process as well as for providing false information in lustration declarations.

Several other draft laws were proposed as an alternative to the *Svoboda* draft. One prepared by the representatives of Yulia Tymoshenko's *Batkivshchyna* party,[26] one by the representatives of Vitaly Klitschko's UDAR,[27] and one by a combined team of *Batkivshchyna* and UDAR MPs.[28] All three alternative proposals were similar to the initial draft in terms of understanding the main goal of lustration (along with the "standard" argument about the need of restoration of trust, the draft laws aimed at fighting crimes against the state and constitutional order, humanity and the rule of law; protecting democracy, the rule of law and basic freedoms). In terms of general categories of persons falling under lustration, alternative drafts were either similar to *Svoboda's* proposal (draft by *Batkivshchyna*), limited only to officials being in office during the Euromaidan events (draft by UDAR) or focusing not only on the period of Viktor Yanukovych's presidency, but also on the second term of Leonid Kuchma which preceded the Orange Revolution (joint draft by Batkivshchyna and UDAR). Neither proposal included the idea of introducing criminal responsibility as a part of the lustration process.

None of these draft laws were voted on, yet the presented proposals provide a basis for an active discussion on how the final design of Ukraine's vetting policy should look like. The differentiation of ideas included in the first drafts submitted in the parliament prove that along with an attempt to meet the obvious social demands to "reboot the authorities", the parties considered lustration as a tool of political struggle. Presenting the most restrictive proposal, the *Svoboda* party was, most probably, aware of small chances for the draft law to be accepted by the parliament that was elected in 2012, the same that provided a necessary majority to Viktor Yanukovych. Being a right-wing party, *Svoboda* has a natural limit of support in the politically diversified Ukrainian society, focused mainly

26 Draft law 'On lustration in Ukraine', no. 4570-1, registered 08 April 2014.
27 Draft law 'On carrying out lustration in Ukraine', no. 4570-3, registered 08 April 2014.
28 Draft law 'On lustration in Ukraine', no. 4570-2, registered 08 April 2014.

in the western regions of the country. So opting for a restrictive vetting policy is in its best interest – it reassures the core electorate of the party and additionally provides a possibility to fight the party's political opponents beyond the electoral field. On the other hand, UDAR and *Batkivshchyna*, trying to take the position of centrist parties, naturally opted for a version that would avoid possible tension in the society and at the same time not hamper their attractiveness as potential coalition partners. Hence, the discussed draft laws indicated the boundary conditions for further debate on the final shape of lustration.

In the meantime, the draft law "On government cleansing" was elaborated by the activists of the Civic Lustration Committee. The proposal was supported by representatives of all parties that formed the interim government, the draft was registered at the *Verkhovna Rada* on 24 July 2014. *Svoboda*, *Batkivshchyna* and UDAR withdrew their own bills and the new draft law was finally adopted on 16 September 2014.[29] The law was not accepted with enthusiasm – it gained 231 votes (226 votes needed for a majority) and most of the MPs that formed the parliamentary majority before the Euromaidan predictably did not support it.

The main aim of the law on lustration is to eliminate from public affairs those whose acts or inactivity supported the usurpation of power by Viktor Yanukovych, endangered the national security or enabled lawless violations of human rights and freedoms. The essential mechanics of Ukrainian lustration is quite simple. The law defines several types of "lustrable offences"[30] which eliminate the possibility to hold public office for a period of five or ten years. Decisions made on the basis of the law can be challenged in court. Importantly, an exception is made for elected positions.

The defined lustrable offences are the following. First, holding a public office of the period of at least one year during the presidency of Viktor Yanukovych and not resigning as a result of the developments caused by the Euromaidan. It should be noted that this offence refers also to judges (as well as representatives of law enforcement agencies) who made a decision that later became an object of the amnesty introduced on 21 February 2014 (see chapter 2). Second, being a high-ranked official of the Communist Party or the All-Union Lenin Communist Union of Youth – the only element of Ukrainian lustration that is targeted at the legacy of the Soviet past. Third, the law introduces a ban for cooperation with foreign intelligence services, acting against the national security and territorial

---

29 Law of Ukraine 'On government cleansing (lustration)', no. 1682-VII, adopted 16 September 2014.

30 Monika Nalepa, *Skeletons in the Closet. Transitional Justice in Post-Communist Europe*, (New York: Cambridge University Press, 2010), 83.

integrity of Ukraine, publicly calling for the violation of territorial integrity and sovereignty of Ukraine, or fomenting ethnic strife (an additional measure that is obviously designed to address the problem of separatism in the eastern regions of the country in the aftermath of the Euromaidan, see chapter 5). Finally, the law introduces the so-called "property lustration" – a ban for public officers not able to explain the origin of their assets. Although it is not expressed directly in the regulation, this norm obviously goes beyond the period of Viktor Yanukovych's presidency and is targeted at Ukraine's immanent problem of corruption.

The lustration process is confession-based. This means that those affected first have to affirm that they need to lodge a declaration whether they fulfil the lustration criteria defined by the law. The declaration is later verified by a state institution employing the affected persons. The refusal to submit a declaration is treated as a confession and the respective person then loses his or her job. The overall control over the lustration process is conducted by the Ministry of Justice (which was to be vetted first). Similar declarations should be lodged by persons applying for positions defined by the law (this rule also does not apply to the elected offices).

Summing up, Ukraine's lustration policy has been designed in such a way that it addresses the same wrongdoings as investigations and trials discussed in the previous chapter, although not on a personal but on a systemic level. The logic of the Ukrainian lustration law obviously goes in the direction of treating corruption as a problem that leads to structural economic violence[31] and thus it addresses the clear demand for cleansing the authorities from corruption. This anti-corruption element, the so-called "property lustration" constitutes an interesting novelty in the practice of vetting policies that supplements classical forms of political-administrative justice known from the experience of other post-communist states.

3.4. Effects and challenges

"How can the rule of law be established; how can a young democracy start working, if the ones who are responsible for the protection of the democracy were the

31 See: Lisa Hecht and Sabina Michalowski, 'The Economic and Social Dimension of Transitional Justice', https://www.essex.ac.uk/tjn/documents/TheeconomicandsocialdimensionsofTJ.pdf (accessed 20 November 2015); Ruben Carranza, 'Plunder and Pain: Should Transitional Justice Engage with Corruption and Economic Crimes?', *The International Journal of Transitional Justice*, vol. 2 (2008): 310–330.

first executioners of it?”[32] – Yegor Sobolev asked this rhetorical question when arguing for lustration during a hearing of the Constitutional Court of Ukraine. Like many other proponents of the idea of lustration, in his public speeches Sobolev tends to emphasize this policy’s main function as to protect democracy in the country. Furthermore, Ukrainian activists note that the law on lustration has become the only legal act that brought measurable results in the sense that it has actually led to the removal of a number of officials who actively supported the policies of Viktor Yanukovych and prevented some of them to relocate to other public positions.[33] Yet, the question arise as to what extent do these assessments correspond with reality? Two years after the start of vetting policies in Ukraine, some preliminary conclusions can be made about what has been already achieved.

When it comes to the so-called lustration of judges, the Special Temporary Commission began functioning on 3 July 2014. It received 2,192 requests to screen judges. The Commission initiated 331 detailed screenings which led to the issuance of 63 conclusions, 46 of which included recommendations to dismiss the judges under scrutiny.[34] Yet, only seven judges had been dismissed in January 2016[35] and the next 29 – in September 2016[36] on the basis of the law “On a restoration of trust in judicial power in Ukraine”. One cannot exclude that the reason for such inefficiency is technical – the functioning of the High Council of Justice, the constitutional organ that has the right to legitimise the proposed dismissals so that the whole procedure corresponds with the constitution, has been *de facto* blocked for a period of one year as a result of the same law. The idea to renew the staff of the institution was undoubtedly dictated by the will to minimize resistance from the representatives of the *ancien regime*. In practice, they

---

32 ‘Vystup Yegora Soboleva v Konstytutsiynomu Sudi’, 112.UA, 22 October 2015, http://ua.112.ua/video/vystup-yehora-sobolieva-v-konstytutsiinomu-sudi-175633.html (accessed 30 October 2015).

33 Author’s interview with Oleksandra Drik, representative of the NGO Civic Lustration Committee, April 2015.

34 Source: website of the High Council of Justice of Ukraine, http://www.vru.gov.ua/statistics/47 (accessed 25 March 2016).

35 Source: website of the President of Ukraine, http://www.president.gov.ua/news/prezident-zvilniv-z-posad-chotiroh-suddiv-zokrema-rodiona-ki-36629; http://www.president.gov.ua/news/prezident-zvilniv-za-porushennya-prisyagi-86-suddiv-v-tomu-c-36686 (accessed 25 March 2016).

36 ‘Rada zvilnyla nyzku suddiv za porushennya prysyagy, sered nyh – Volkova’, *Ukrayinska Pravda*, 29 September 2016, http://www.pravda.com.ua/news/2016/09/29/7122128/ (accessed 30 September 2016).

managed to at least block new approvals for quite a significant period of time.[37] In other words, the scale of lustration of the judicial power in Ukraine expressed in quantitative terms is far from astonishing although the final outcome of it will be evident only from the perspective of a more distant future.

As for the law "On cleansing the government", according to information published by the Ministry of Justice of Ukraine, 925 persons had been lustrated by the beginning of June 2016 (the number is constantly growing).[38] Comparing these numbers with some initial declarations of the politicians may be surprising. For example, in September 2014 Prime Minister Yatsenyuk spoke about one million officials who potentially fall under lustration.[39] Much more moderate estimations by the Civic Lustration Committee suggest around 2,600 people should ultimately fall under lustration.[40] Just like in the case of the judges, the process is ongoing and the final number of vetted officials remains unknown. Furthermore, the statistics do not say anything about another important phenomenon – how some officials decided to resign by their own will, if they know that the chances of keeping their position are low.[41] In in any case, one can hardly speak about a massive purge of officials as a result of the major lustration law.

As it was mentioned earlier, Ukrainian vetting policy has faced severe criticism, especially from the side of the representatives from the *ancien regime*. The law on lustration was assessed by the Venice Commission. Although the idea of lustration was accepted in general, the Commission urged the *Verkhovna Rada* to reconsider the scope of vetting, in particular to separate it from anti-corruption measures: "The protection of a newly democratic regime from the elites of the previous non-democratic one and the fight against corruption are both valuable and legitimate political aims. Yet, they can hardly be achieved through the same means." Also, the Commission suggested that "ordinary judges should

---

37 Roman Kuybida, 'Pravo na spravedlyviy sud: inshi aspekty', in *Prava lyudyny v Ukrayini: pershe pivrichchya 2015*, ed. Alla Blaga and Oleg Martynenko (Kyiv: Ukrayinska helsinska spilka z praw lyudyny, 2015), 67.

38 The official public register of lustrated persons is available online: http://lustration.minjust.gov.ua/register.

39 'Pid lyustratsiyu pidpadaye blyzko milyona chynovnykiv ta pravoohorontsiv – Yastenyuk', UNIAN, 17 September 2014, http://www.unian.ua/politics/985921-pid-lyustratsiyu-pidpadae-blizko-milyona-chinovnikiv-ta-pravoohorontsiv-yatsenyuk.html (accessed 20 September 2014).

40 The register prepared by the Civic Lustration Committee is available online: http://lku.org.ua/registry/dashboard.

41 Author's interview with Oleksandra Drik, April 2015.

be excluded [...] and subject solely to the regime of the Law on the restoration of trust in the judiciary of Ukraine", and that the policy in general should be put under the supervision of an independent institution rather than the Ministry of Justice.[42]

The most important arguments against lustration have been formulated in three complaints that have been submitted to the Constitutional Court of Ukraine aimed at annulment of the core provisions of the law "On cleansing the government". Two complaints have been prepared by the Supreme Court of Ukraine (SCU); one is authored by a group of 47 MPs, representing mainly the remnants of Yanukovych's Party of Regions. As one might expect, the proponents of lustration characterize the complaints as political steps undertaken by the *ancien regime* either openly (through MPs) or by the "bad social capital" within the judiciary under the cover of one of the key institutions within the system (through the SCU) in order to undermine the idea of lustration as such. Although it is hard not to agree with these arguments, the complaints themselves obviously deserve attention as they cannot be ignored by a political regime that emphasizes its commitments to democratic values. The first of the complaints (submitted by the SCU on 17 November 2014) was obviously focused on "protecting" the judiciary. It highlights three doubts: the lustration procedures do not guarantee an individual approach to each case (and thus *de facto* establishes collective responsibility); judges who issued verdicts during the Euromaidan protests did so in accordance with the law (and thus there is no ground to speak about breaking the judicial oath); and no one can be brought to justice twice for the same deed (and, as we remember, judges were affected by both vetting laws). On 16 March 2015, the SCU in its second complaint extended the number of doubts and provided the following arguments: the law on lustration introduces *de facto* discrimination of certain categories of citizens willing to enter public service (thus the principle of equality in access to public service is violated); the law introduces a new type of legal responsibility that does not require proving of individual guilt; the law introduces *de facto* punishment without court decisions (in other words, the SCU regards lustration in general as punishment, and the procedure as introducing the unacceptable presumption of guilt); and that the legal responsibility introduced by the law is retrospective in nature. Another complaint submitted by a group of parliamentarians on 20 January 2015 is more extensive. It repeats

42 European Commission for Democracy through Law (Venice Commission), *Final Opinion on the Law on Government Cleansing (Lustration Law) of Ukraine*, Venice 19 June 2015, Opinion no. 788/2014.

some of the already-mentioned arguments, but also introduces new ones: the inadmissibility of collective responsibility, a *de facto* presumption of guilt and retrospective justice (in this complaint the argument refers also to the so-called "property lustration"); an insufficient protection of honour and dignity of the affected persons; the authors repeat the arguments that no one can be brought to justice twice and that decisions of judges during the Euromaidan were lawful. In addition, the authors provide two unconventional arguments – that the lustration introduces discrimination in access to certain types of jobs and that lustration of former communist officials limits ideological and political plurality. The CCU combined all three complaints into one case, the date of issuing the final verdict remains unknown at the time of writing.

It is not the aim here to assess whether the accepted and implemented design of the policy corresponds with Ukraine's constitution. Clearly, the legal doubts expressed in the constitutional complaints are not specific for the Ukrainian case as most of them have been discussed in the first part of this chapter. Nevertheless, the main arguments that might support a continuation of Ukraine's lustration should be reiterated. Transitional justice in general and vetting policies in particular are extraordinary in nature, which usually means a conscious adding of a political layer to "normal" justice. This is undoubtedly incompatible with the rule of law in "ordinary" times, but may be acceptable in cases when the goal is to strengthen the regime that is committed to establishing the rule of law. In other words, the main question here is not whether the design of the policy corresponds with the principle of the rule of law (it does not), but whether the exceptions introduced by the policy are subject to some rules, whether they do not allow for purely arbitrary decisions, and what are the acceptable limits of these rules from the perspective of Ukraine's newly established political regime. The verdict of the CCU is actually desirable, as it should provide definite answers to these questions and doubts. The only significant doubt that remains, however, is the level of independence of the CCU itself.

It is evident that the judiciary has become a significant player with a potential to limit and even cancel Ukraine's lustration policy. This might not rise controversy if we deal with a consolidated democratic political system. In the conditions of Ukraine's transitions, however, things look more nuanced. In particular one should take into account the criminal proceedings that have been initiated including against the judges of the CCU who remained in office while working on the mentioned complaints questioning provisions of the law on lustration. Additionally, some of these judges also fall under the provisions of the law on lustration. Thus, a clear possibility opens for both the government and the CCU to exert pressure on each other: the government may "remind" the judges about ongoing criminal cases in order to gain the most desirable verdict and the court can "remind" the government that it can induce public dissatisfaction by *de facto* cancelling vetting policies. Generally, no matter what shape the CCU's verdict will take, there is a large field for speculation as to whether the decision is motivated by a genuine care to support the rule of law.

Even without the most significant verdict by the CCU, the right to appeal, has established a link between both elements of Ukraine's vetting policies. About half of lustrated persons challenge the decision in court.[43] Furthermore, the role of the judiciary becomes even clearer if one takes into account that the court verdict is actually necessary in the case of some lustrable offences defined by the law: public calls for violence or violation of territorial integrity as well as corruption are crimes and thus should be proven in court in each particular case. This means that the judiciary has gained a significant leverage on the effects of the policy even without the change of provisions in the law. Indeed, using courts (which, as we remember has not been "cleansed") to undermine the lustration decisions was marked as one of the main ways to obstruct the law in the report summing up the first year of implementation of the policy.[44] Obviously, doubts may appear in the public sphere as to what extent such decisions are "just".

Along with the doubts that are of legal (and to some extent even philosophical) nature, several important issues have risen referring to the practice of the implementation of the policy. In particular, doubts have been expressed about whether lustration would not undermine the governance capacity of the state.[45] Indeed, such problem appeared in the field of defence – the highest military officials also fell under lustration, which was quickly recognized as a potential threat in the conditions of the ongoing military conflict in Donbas. In January 2015, the law on lustration was amended allowing the President to "shield" officers from lustration.[46]

The report on the first year of implementation has also noted some significant violations of the law including a loose interpretation of the law by particular institutions, obtaining by officials subject to lustration of the status of anti-terrorist

---

43 Author's interview with Oleksandra Drik, April 2015.

44 Civic Lustration Committee, *Rik lyustratsiyi v Ukrayini: istoriya peremoh ta sabotazhu*, (Kyiv, 2015).

45 Aleksey Volkov, 'Lyustratsiya ili kastratsiya?', *Zerkalo Nedeli*, 29 May 2015.

46 Law of Ukraine 'On amendment to the Law of Ukraine "On government cleansing" regarding additional measures to ensure the defence capability of the state', no. 132-VIII, adopted 27 January 2015.

operation participant (see chapter 5), guaranteeing of immunity from lustration, and abuse and even unconcealed ignoring of the law.[47] In other words there is a strong resistance from the side of the authorities (especially visible in the lustration of judges) and bureaucracy which reflects the insufficient capacity of the state to implement such a policy.

The decisions on the removal of officials on the basis of the law on lustration are often arbitrary. "Once again, we see the same selectivity and the use [of the policy] to eliminate 'the undesirable ones'. Meanwhile, officials with considerable assets usually avoid lustration. There is a common injustice that causes sad laughter among the majority of civil servants with whom I communicate. It all happens when salaries of civil servants are miserable and the ones who call for lustration have several times bigger incomes"[48] – such a poignant assessment of lustration, in particular of its assets-control element, has been presented to the author by a Ukrainian civil servant who has gone through the procedure of screening. Of course, one such voice is not necessarily representative and it indicates a new research question that can be answered only when all the procedures connected with the lustration are complete. Nevertheless, this perspective should be taken into account since accusations of a selective application of the law have been publicly expressed to the president from others as well, including the head of department in the Ministry of Justice responsible for implementation the lustration.[49] Such problems obviously do not contribute to strengthening the perception of the state as devoid of patrimony.

Finally, there is a doubt of less importance, though stressed by the Venice Commission – how does including anti-communist measures 25 years later help to protect democracy? The Communist Party of Ukraine lost its political appeal and ceased to be a significant player on the country's political arena. Obviously, it will not bring a retrospective solution to the genuine problem of post-1991 role of former communists in building a system of "oligarchic democracy". Probably, it would be better to put it into the category of so-called "historical justice" – a policy that will be discussed in the following chapter.

47 Civic Lustration Committee, supra n 44.

48 Author's interview with Ukrainian civil servant of the middle level, who has gone through the process of screening, February 2016.

49 'Holovnyy lyustrator doriknula Poroshenkovi nezvilnennyam suddiv KS', *Ukrayinska Pravda*, 21 March 2016, http://www.pravda.com.ua/news/2016/03/21/7102800/ (accessed 17 May 2016).

4. Historical justice

4.1. Theoretical background

Along with investigations and trials, as well as vetting policies, all of which are targeted at the legacy of the recent past, Ukraine's post-Euromaidan authorities have initiated a policy addressed at the more distant Soviet past. As described in chapter 3, the logic of Ukrainian lustration policy has been refocused away from the Soviet legacy, as it was proposed in some lustration projects after the Orange revolution. As a result, Ukrainian lustration differs from vetting policies implemented in other post-communist countries. Banning former communist *apparatchiks* from access to public offices a quarter of a century after the transition in 1991 is rather an addition to Ukrainian lustration, not the essence of it. However, it does not change the fact that the Ukrainian public space remains full of symbolic reminders of the communist past (from names of cities, towns and villages, to some state rituals, such as the way of celebrating the Victory Day on 9 May). Some of these symbols have been organically modernized and were used by politicians appealing to the part of society characterized by nostalgia for the Soviet past in order to build specific "ecological niches" of core electorates. It refers especially to the business-political "Donetsk clan", which obtained full domination over Ukrainian politics when Viktor Yanukovych was elected to the presidency in 2010. Ultimately, such nursing of Soviet traditions contributed to the maintenance of the specific self-identification of inhabitants of the eastern regions of the country and thus created favourable conditions for the outbreak of the conflict, which will be discussed in details in the following chapter.

The symbolic policy which deals with the exclusion of certain values and attitudes is thus targeted not only at the Soviet legacy as these values are associated with the legacy of the Yanukovych regime as well. Unlike the policies of transitional justice described in previous chapters, this policy does not target any particular individual deeds (like criminal justice) or particular categories of current or potential state officials (like vetting); instead, it consists of the public blaming and shaming of institutions, persons and cultural phenomena, which are now regarded as emanations of a bad past, endangering the reconstruction of the country and the proliferation of democratic, pluralist and pro-Western values. This can be called dealing with the past with the aim of symbolically breaking with the former political regimes.

To a large extent, this dimension of transitional justice in Ukraine is close to what Ruti Teitel calls historical justice, a "historical response to evil legacies" that is based on the assumption that "establishing the 'truth' about the state's past wrongs [...] can serve to lay the foundation of the new political order".[1] In other words, the policy of historical justice is aimed at opening a way for telling the "truth" about the wrongdoings of the *ancien regime*. The word "truth" is put in quotation marks on purpose, for it may not necessarily lead to the reconstruction of an objective picture of reality under the *ancien regime*. A philosopher might say that the very notions of truth and objectivity are far from being obvious. Therefore, from the perspective of historical justice it might be more correct (and less controversial) to speak about a point of view on the past that is alternative to the one endorsed by the *ancien regime*. Especially if we take into consideration the fact that the most serious wrongdoings conducted by the Soviet regime predominantly belong to a distant past, there is no possibility to rest upon testimonies of witnesses to tell objective "truth" about the past. Therefore, from the perspective of the overriding topic of the book, it would be more accurate to speak about different narratives interpreting historic events. In practical terms, the policy of historical justice may take the form of the state creating conditions for a free deliberation about the interpretation of the past, both among politicians and scientists, that might lead to a consensus in this field (a kind of bottom-up approach one can expect to be applied by more liberal regimes). On the other hand, the incoming regime may simply introduce a new official narrative containing certain, clearly defined interpretations of the past (a kind of top-down approach that may be more typical to less liberal political regimes, tending to authoritarianism). One can assume that in order to achieve the goal of a symbolic break with the past, the combination of both approaches can be applied. Without free deliberation it is hard to expect that the new interpretation of the past is accepted by the society without resistance; at the same time, it is easy to imagine that the state draws official limits for such deliberations in order to eliminate extremist points of view – consider the illegality of Holocaust denial in some countries as an example of such limits.

Thus, one can assume that the practical reason to introduce policies of historical justice is not to find "truth", but rather to eliminate (or at least limit) the influence of the values on which the *ancien regime* was based. This function is similar to the function of vetting. The difference is in the speed of change induced by the policy: while vetting allows the removal of the bearers of unwanted values from the state apparatus relatively quickly, it takes a much longer time to delegitimise ideas in the eyes of public opinion. It is also important to note that the success

1 Ruti G. Teitel, *Transitional Justice*, (New York: Oxford University Press, 2000), 69.

of historical justice policies in achieving their goals may depend on the effects of other transitional justice mechanisms: trials and vetting may provide the incoming regime with evidence supporting the new preferable narrative about the past.

An impact of historical justice policies on the political development will thus depend on what kind of values are regarded as unwanted, which ones are endorsed, whether there is a coherence between the promoted values and the actual deeds of the authorities. Unlike in the case of other transitional justice mechanisms, there will be much less immediately visible effects. The intuitive expectation towards the policies of reformulation of public memory is that by revealing the facts about past wrongdoings, a reconciliation may be achieved. The literature refers mainly to cases where such mechanisms (for example truth commissions) constitute the core of transitional justice efforts.[2] At the same time, like other transitional justice mechanisms, historical justice has a significant potential for generating conflicts. "The turn to the law to protect a particular historical account can occasion profound dilemmas, because such regulation often competes with other societal interests associated with the liberal state, such as unbounded freedom of expression".[3] In other words, the effects of the implementation of policies that fit into the category of historical justice may also contribute to political decay of the state. Having stated so, I will turn to the analysis of the attitude of Ukrainians to the Soviet past: To which extent the values and traditions that can be regarded as an emanation of the Soviet past, inherited by the post-1991 Ukraine, are regarded as a potential obstacle for the proliferation of democratic, pro-Western values? Whether the implemented policies correspond with actual political demand in this field?

4.2. Demand: the attitude of Ukrainians to the Soviet past

The role of the Soviet period in the history of Ukraine is ambiguous. On the one hand, it is associated with a large scale of violence. Several million Ukrainians became victims of the Holodomor, a famine caused by the Soviet policy of collectivisation in 1932–1933. Ukrainians, in particular inhabitants of the western regions of the country which were incorporated into the USSR in 1939 according

---

2 On the other side, there are voices sceptical about such function of truth-seeking policies: Erin Daly, "Truth Scepticism: An Inquiry into the Value of Truth in Times of Transition", *The international Journal of Transitional Justice*, Vol. 2, 2008; David Rieff, *In Praising of Forgetting. Historical Memory and its Ironies*, (New Haven and London: Yale University Press, 2015).

3 Teitel, supra n 1 at 108.

to the Ribbentrop-Molotov pact, became targets of severe political repressions. In the post-Stalin period, the scale of repressions decreased, but they were targeted at any manifestation of independent thought, which was almost automatically labelled as "nationalist". On the other hand, although the Soviet Union is primarily the emanation of Russian statehood, Ukrainians were "co-owners" of it. Ukrainians were not banned from careers; repressions, especially in the post-war period, did not have an ethnic nature. Consequently, the Soviet rule was not regarded by a significant proportion of the population as a period of foreign domination, with the exception of the mentioned western regions of Ukraine, which had much less common history with the Russian empire and its Soviet continuation. Moreover, the overwhelming support for independence in 1991 was not dictated by the motivation to obtain freedom from foreign oppression but rather by pragmatic calculations that an independent Ukraine may appear better in maintaining the socio-economic status of its citizenry than the Soviet Union with its declining economy. In other words, the perception of the Soviet past is different from what is typically found in the Central European or Baltic states – there is a much deeper feeling of "ownership" of that past.

The historical background has conditioned a specific duality for the Ukrainian identity. While the majority of inhabitants of Ukraine consequently identify themselves as Ukrainians (and so identify themselves with the state they live in), there are noticeable differences in attitudes to the problems of the past, present and future between eastern and western regions of Ukraine. It should be clearly stressed here that a division of Ukraine into two major political-cultural entities is a serious oversimplification, which is popular thanks in part to the media that often refer to this division in simplistic terms ("pro-Russian east" vs. "pro-European west"). Neither the west nor east of Ukraine can be fully described using such a one-dimensional tool of measuring attitudes. Nevertheless, at a certain level of generalisation one can legitimately say that the "contemporary post-Soviet Ukraine is a battlefield between two versions of Ukrainian history: The Soviet version and the traditional Ukrainian one. One can say that both versions have a clear 'regional scope', and that one of them is more eastern and another one is more western".[4]

As it was mentioned in the previous chapters, before 2014 the issue of dealing with the Soviet past could be regarded as purely theoretical. It was a topic discussed in closed circles of academics and intellectuals, but had not become

4 Jarosław Hrycak, *Nowa Ukraina. Nowe interpretacje*, (Wrocław: College of Eastern Europe, 2009), 146.

a major political issue. There were some prominent exceptions, however. One of them was during the presidential campaign in 1999, when Leonid Kuchma was re-elected thanks to the fact that in the second round of election he faced Petro Symonenko, the leader of the Communist Party of Ukraine (CPU). This manoeuvre allowed Kuchma, himself a former "red director",[5] to persuade the Soviet-sceptic regions to vote for him as a "lesser evil". Examples like this prove that an adequate use of post-Soviet sentiments can bring tangible political results. Such instances, however, were sporadic; there remained a significant gap in dealing with the Soviet past in general. Several surveys, conducted in the 2000s may show the cause of such state of affairs – the majority of Ukrainians believed that the best way to deal with the past violence is to "consider that no one was right or wrong" (Figure 3). One should note, however, that the proportion of the ones convinced that the ones responsible for past violence should be punished grew as the Soviet past became more distant.

Figure 3: Attitude of Ukrainians to responsibility for historic wrongdoings

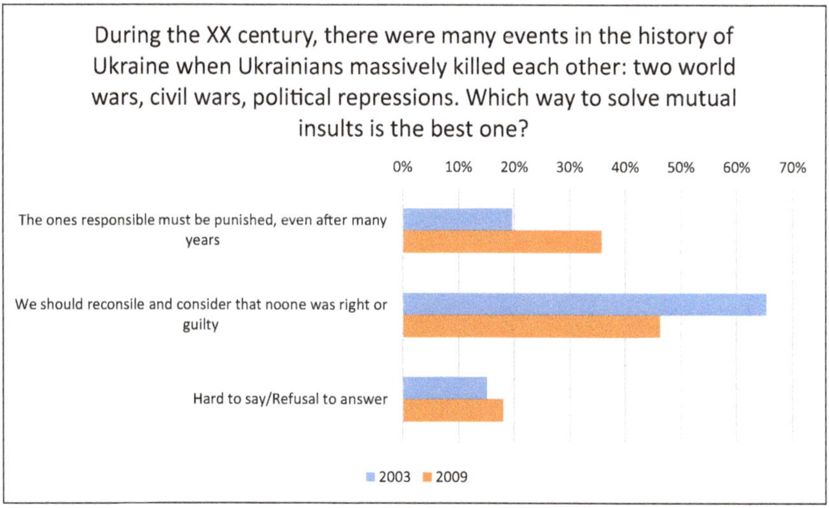

Source: Razumkov Centre, http://www.razumkov.org.ua/ukr/poll.php?poll_id=454 (accessed 10 April 2016).

5 The term used to describe directors of state enterprises, who started managing the companies in the Soviet times and continued running them after the transition. The notion suggests close relations with the party, because political loyalty was undoubtedly one of the criterions of such nominations.

The change in attitudes towards specific Soviet subjects is reflected in other data, such as the survey measuring the approach to the celebration of the Day of the October Revolution. The number of supporters of that holiday has decreased by 40 percent between 2002 and 2009. What is not less important, this decrease did not go in parallel with the change on the opposite side of the continuum of perception of Soviet past – the number of people, for whom one of the biggest communist holidays is the occasion to commemorate the memory of the victims of the Soviet regime, hasn't changed (Figure 4).

Figure 4: Perception of the day of October Revolution

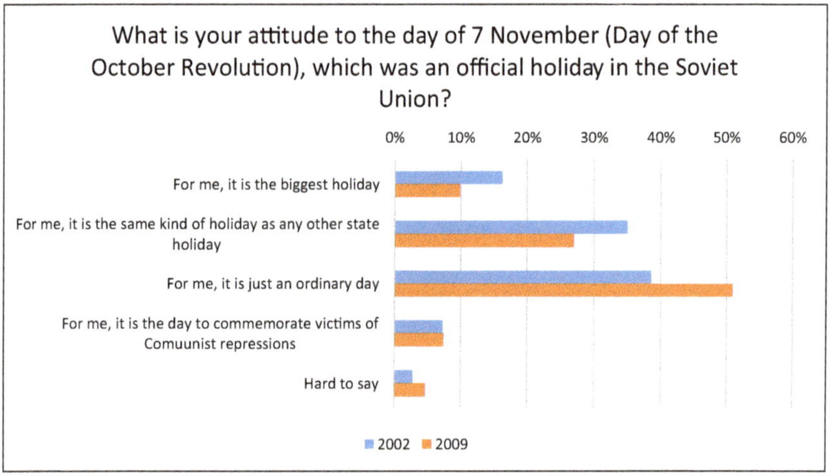

Source: Razumkov Centre, http://www.razumkov.org.ua/ukr/poll.php?poll_id=503 (accessed 10 April 2016).

The mentioned regional disproportions are reflected in Figure 5. As we can see, although there is an obvious difference in attitudes to the idea of erecting of Stalin monuments, it is expressed mainly in the number of opponents; east and west are not "mirror reflections" of each other.

Figure 5: Regional disparities in attitudes to commemorating Joseph Stalin (April 2010)

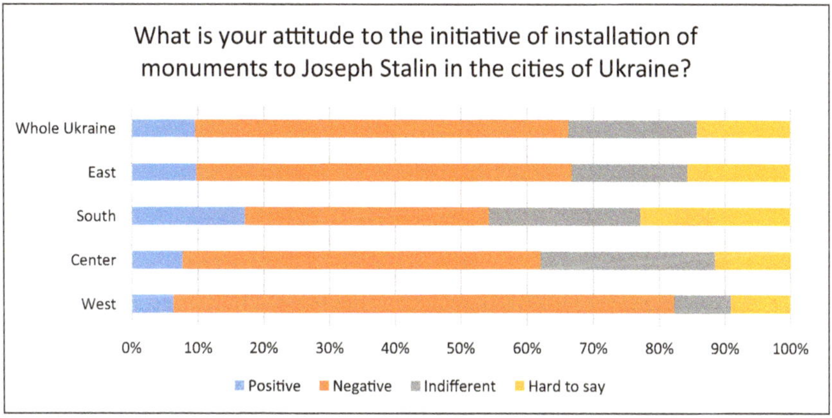

Source: Razumkov Centre, http://www.razumkov.org.ua/ukr/poll.php?poll_id=547 (accessed 10 April 2016).

Although the Euromaidan protests were aimed not against the Soviet legacy, but against much more contemporary problems associated with the system of "oligarchic democracy", toppling Lenin monuments became one of the symbols of the notorious movement. The most well-known monument situated in the centre of Kyiv was downed on 8 December 2013, triggering the so-called *leninopad* (the fall of Lenin) throughout the whole country. Just like the case of transitional justice policies discussed in chapters 2 and 3, demolishing Soviet monuments was promoted primarily by a narrow group of activists who saw a clear association between the Soviet past and the post-Soviet political development of the country. Whether it was a symptom of growing popularity of the idea of de-communisation remains questionable. Rather, they should be regarded as spontaneous acts performed by the most active opponents of the communists accompanied by the indifference of the society as a whole. The issue of de-communisation traditionally has been passed over during two national electoral campaigns that happened after the Euromaidan; also the effects of the de-communisation law (which will be discussed below) was not met with high enthusiasm. Indeed, a survey conducted after the Euromaidan, at the end of 2014–beginning of 2015,[6] has revealed

6 Democratic Initiatives Foundations, 'Shcho ob'yednuye ta roz'yednuye ukrayintsiv', http://dif.org.ua/ua/publications/press-relizy/sho-obednue-ta-rozednue-ukrainciv.htm (accessed 20 April 2016).

some interesting details. The overall picture remained quite similar to the one we could observe before the Euromaidan. In most regions of Ukraine, the majority of the population has a positive attitude to the dissolution of the USSR in 1991. Also the Euromaidan—the most recent historical event—has proven to be perceived predominantly positive throughout the country.[7] The most interesting observation that comes out of the cited research is the fact that public attitudes to different aspects of the Soviet past do not have a potential to become significant dividing factors; instead the aspects of what was called by Yaroslav Hrytsak the traditional Ukrainian history do have such a potential. In particular, inhabitants of the East are not ready to accept the "western" version of history. Just like in the Soviet times, this version of Ukrainian history is almost automatically referred to as "nationalist" and even "radical".[8]

Another important phenomenon that was highlighted by the survey is that among the factors that may appear crucial for reconciliation in Ukraine (one should remember that the study was conducted in the conditions of *de facto* war), inhabitants of most regions of Ukraine name: victory in the war; the effective fight against corruption; and an improvement in the social and economic situation in the country. None of the top responses here would fit into the wider category of historical justice. Truth be told, most of the surveys are constructed in such a way that allows an assessment of the relative importance of different social and political issues in the eyes of the public opinion (some of which are cited in this book), conducted either before or after the Euromaidan, simply do not mention issues that refer to any kind of symbolic break with the past. The obvious reason for this is that scholars themselves do not regard these issues as the ones that define the essence of political debate in the country. In sum, there is no reason to think that the Euromaidan has induced a significant level of demand for a policy leading to a symbolic break with the past. What has changed, however, is that the protests of 2013–2014 have brought a reshuffle in the political elites of the country, making the voice of the proponents of the policy much more resonant.

---

7 One should take into account, however, that the survey did not cover Crimea and territories in Donbas occupied by the so-called "people's republics". Therefore, the results may be distorted.

8 The specificity of Donbas's perception of Ukraine's contemporary reality is discussed in chapter 5.

4.3. Supply: design of historical justice policies

After 1991 several steps have been made in Ukraine which could fit into the category of historical justice. As early as 17 April 1991, the law "On the rehabilitation of victims of political repressions in Ukraine" has been adopted.[9] According to the law, the *Verkhovna Rada* "dissociated itself from terrorist methods of management of society" and proclaimed condemnation of political repressions that took place under Soviet rule. Additionally, the law obliged the state to pay compensation to rehabilitated persons. On the other hand, the act has not condemned the nature of the communist regime as such – it was focused on "unlawful repressions". By the year 2001, rehabilitation was granted to 248,710 persons, while 117,243 applications were rejected.[10]

Simultaneously, the Ukrainian authorities began a process of opening and facilitating access to declassified Soviet documents. On 6 April 1992, the *Verkhovna Rada* adopted a resolution on the preparation of a multi-volume scientific publication documenting the victims of repression in Ukraine.[11] In September 1992, the government established the editorial board of the publishing series titled "Rehabilitated by History" (Ukr.: *Реабілітовані історією*).[12] Along with the implementation of the task of issuing the scientific publication, the board later became responsible for the functioning of the online database "National Bank of the Repressed" (Ukr.: *Національний банк репресованих*), which is formed on the basis of lists of persons in the published volumes of "Rehabilitated by History".[13] These measures, however, do not exactly fit the pattern of truth-revelation policies known from other post-communist states, since the ones in Ukraine focused exclusively on victims of the regime and did not reveal much about the ones responsible for the implementation of the repressions.

---

9 Law of Ukraine 'On the rehabilitation of victims of political repressions in Ukraine', no. 962-XII, adopted 17 April 1991.

10 Security Service of Ukraine, 'Uchast' Sluzhby Bezpeky Ukrayiny u reabilitatsiyi zhertv politychnyh represiy v Ukrayini', http://www.sbu.gov.ua/sbu/control/uk/publish/article;jsessionid=59BC41CD4DC2328F115AC76B60B5F646?art_id=49641&cat_id=49348 (accessed 20 April 2016).

11 Decree of the Presidium of the Verkhovna Rada of Ukraine, 'On preparation of the multi-volume scientific documentary publication on the victims of political repressions in Ukraine', no. 2256-XII, adopted 6 April 1992.

12 Decree of the Cabinet of Ministers of Ukraine 'On preparation and publishing of a series of books "Rehabilitated by History"', no. 530, adopted 11 September 1992.

13 The database is available online: http://www.reabit.org.ua/nbr/.

Some additional steps to push the policy of historical justice forward, in particular towards a condemnation of the communist regime as such, were done under the presidency of Viktor Yushchenko. Being fond of history, Yushchenko devoted much time to popularize knowledge about one of the most tragic events in the history of Ukraine – the already-mentioned Holodomor. In 2006 the *Verkhovna Rada* adopted a law that recognised the Holodomor of 1932–1933 as a genocide against the Ukrainian people,[14] thus moving much farther than speaking about merely "unlawful repressions" conducted by the Soviet authorities. Consequently, the commemoration of the 75th anniversary of Holodomor in November 2007 became a large and widely-promoted event. Within the package of measures prepared for the anniversary, a new online database was created titled "Ukrainian Martyrdom of the 20th Century" (Ukr.: *Український мартиролог XX ст.*), with the aim of publishing photos and brief biographical information about the victims of political repressions in 1920–1950.[15] Similar to the "National Bank of the Repressed", this database only tells the stories of victims of political violence committed by the Soviet authorities. Yushchenko's focus on the period of Stalinism, during which the most violent repressions, and even acts of genocide (Holodomor), took place, had a practical political value. It was meant to build a foundation for a national myth that would not divide the different parts of Ukrainian society, taking into account that the tragedy of Holodomor is relevant basically to all of Ukraine, not a specific region of the country. Another important achievement of Yushchenko's presidency in this field was the establishment of the Ukrainian Institute for National Memory (UINM) in May 2006 with the status of a central executive body aimed at restoration and preservation of the national memory of the Ukrainian people.[16] The Institute was closed after Yanukovych came to power in 2010.[17] President Yanukovych ordered a new institution be created with the same name but with a different (lower) status – as a research unit within the structure of government.[18]

14 Law of Ukraine 'On Holodomor of 1932–1933 in Ukraine', no. 376-V, adopted 28 November 2006.

15 The database is available online: http://www.archives.gov.ua/Sections/Martyrolog/.

16 Decree of the Cabinet of Ministers of Ukraine 'On creation of the Ukrainian Institute of National Memory', no. 764, adopted 31 May 2006.

17 Decree of the President of Ukraine 'On optimisation of the system of executive bodies', no. 1085/2010, 9 December 2010.

18 Decree of the President of Ukraine 'The issue of the Ukrainian Institute of National Memory', no. 1086/2010, 9 December 2010.

The Euromaidan protest, in particular the enthusiasm of the anti-communist activists has given the Ukrainian policy of historical justice new life. As the first step in this field, the UINM was recreated in November 2014 as an institution of executive power, the activity of which is directed and coordinated by the Cabinet of Ministers of Ukraine through the Minister of Culture, and the main goal of which is to implement state policy in the field of restoration and preservation of national memory of the Ukrainian people.[19] The Institute was headed by a young historian, Volodymyr Vyatrovych, known for his strong anti-Communist views.

Furthermore, in April 2015, a package of four ambitious laws (popularly called the "de-communisation laws") was adopted by the parliament, marking a new stage in the development of the policy of historical justice. In particular, the Ukrainian state has obviously declared its will not only to commemorate victims of the communist past, but also to conduct an active historical policy. The most significant of the mentioned laws is the one "On the condemnation of communist and national-socialist totalitarian regimes in Ukraine and the prohibition of promotion of their symbols".[20] As it can be deduced from the very title of the regulation, its common name referring only to de-communisation is misleading, because of the law's dual focus on both Soviet and Nazi ideologies, which makes it similar to the policies of historical justice in the Baltic states.[21] In practice, however, the de-communisation element is obviously much more important because of the widespread presence of Soviet symbols in the Ukrainian public space. The law announces that the "Communist totalitarian regime of 1917–1991 is recognized as a criminal one, and one that utilized the policy of state terror characterized by mass violations of human rights [...], and thus is condemned as incompatible with the basic rights and freedoms of man and citizen". The law has obliged the state to investigate the crimes of genocide, crimes against humanity and war crimes committed on the territory of Ukraine by representatives of both communist and Nazi regimes, in order to "restore historical justice".

19 Decree of the Cabinet of Ministers of Ukraine 'Some issues related to the Ukrainian Institute of National Memory', no. 684, adopted 12 November 2014.

20 Law of Ukraine 'On the condemnation of communist and national-socialist totalitarian regimes in Ukraine and prohibition of promotion of their symbols', no. 317-VIII, adopted 9 April 2015.

21 Andrew H. Beattie, 'Post-Communist Truth Commissions: Between Transitional Justice and the Politics of History', in *Post-Communist Transitional Justice. Lessons from Twenty-Five Years of Experience*, ed. Lavinia Stan and Nadya Nedelsky (New York: Cambridge University Press, 2015), 222.

In practical terms, the law established the prohibition to use both communist and Nazi symbols except from educational and scientific purposes. Furthermore, the law obliged local authorities to demount all monuments of communist leaders and, most importantly, to rename all topographic names that refer to the Soviet past. The process of changing topographic names should include public hearings, so that the decision about the new name was accepted by the affected community. The UINM has been given an advisory and recommendation role in this process. In the case where the local authorities fail to propose acceptable changes, appropriate decisions are to be made by the parliament on the basis of recommendations provided by the UINM. The whole process should end within the period of one year since the law entered into force (21 May 2015). Importantly, the law introduced criminal responsibility for violating its provisions. The law has been assessed by the Venice Commission, which accepted it as the one "pursuing legitimate aims", but recommended introducing several amendments. The most significant include: a clearer definition of the notion of propaganda and rethinking the scale of sanctions introduced by the law ("a mere display of a symbol or use of a name should not result in imprisonment").[22]

The second law in the package is one regarding opening access to the archives of organs of repression of the communist totalitarian regime.[23] The law admits that "a better understanding of the newest history can contribute to avoidance of conflict and the hostility in the society" and that the "inaccessibility to the archives has become one of the prerequisites of the annexation of the Crimean Peninsula and of the armed conflict in the territory of Donetsk and Luhansk oblasts". The basic principle introduced by the law, and which differentiates it from the previously-mentioned initiatives implemented in the 1990s and 2000s, is that the information about staff and collaborators of the repressive bodies of the Soviet regime is open, and access to this information cannot be restricted. It is therefore an important step which complements the element of lustration policy targeted at former Soviet officials. Additionally, the law established a basis to establish a Specialized State Archive of the UINM as the principal provider of public access to archive information. The archives being at the disposal of particular ministries and executive bodies, which are assignees of the Soviet repressive bodies,

22 European Commission for Democracy through Law, 'Joint Interim opinion on the law of Ukraine On the condemnation of the Communist and National Socialist (Nazi) regimes and prohibition of propaganda of their symbols', no. CDL-AD(2015)041, 21 December 2015.

23 Law of Ukraine 'On the access to archives of the repressive bodies of the Communist totalitarian regime of 1917–1991', no. 316-VIII, adopted 9 April 2015.

are obliged to transfer the materials referring to the period of 1917–1991 to the UINM within the period of two years since the law enters into force. At the moment of writing the book (about one year after the discussed law entered into force), the Archive has not yet been established, the Institute was seeking the necessary resources.[24] One should note, however, that although the law should be regarded as a step towards genuine openness of Soviet-period documents, the main archives remain in Moscow, where access to them has become rather harder,[25] and thus will remain inaccessible to Ukrainian citizens.

The remaining two laws adopted on 9 April 2015 have a slightly different function – they show an attempt to establish a new official narrative interpreting historical facts. The law "On the legal status and commemoration of the memory of fighters for the independence of Ukraine in the 20th century"[26] is aimed at recognition of all the organisations that acted before 24 August 1991 in the name of restoration of independence of Ukraine (thus the ones who were claimed to be "nationalists" in the Soviet narratives). The law mandates that the state provide conditions for comprehensive research into the history of struggle for independence and introduced the basis for legal prosecution of the ones who publicly reject the legality of Ukrainian's fight for independence in the 20th century. The provision on penalization, however, is formulated in a very general and even vague manner, which makes it challenging to be implemented. It should be noted, that this law received the most criticism due to its explicit mentioning of the Ukrainian Insurgent Army (UPA) among the organisation praised by the law. The UPA has been described in Soviet, as well as Russian historiography, as Nazi collaborators and war criminals. It is also regarded as the perpetrator of genocide against the Polish population of the Volhynia (Wołyń) region in 1943–1944 by Polish historians. In combination with the possibility of legal prosecution opened by the law, this fact has been interpreted in such a way that it might *de facto* lead to a limitation in the freedom of scientific research, leaving space for only one narrative interpreting historical facts.[27] From the perspective of one year of implementation of the law, it

24 Volodymyr Vyatrovych, 'Vozvrashchaem lyudyam istoriyu, istorii vozvrashchaem lyudey', *Zerkalo Nedeli*, 1 April 2016.

25 Ilan Berman, 'Closing the Archives. What Russia's Renewed Secrecy Says about Putin', *Foreign Affairs*, 24 April 2016.

26 Law of Ukraine 'On the legal status and commemoration of the memory of fighters for the independence of Ukraine in the twentieth century', no. 314-VIII, adopted 9 April 2015.

27 For example: Josh Cohen, 'The Historian Whitewashing Ukraine's Past', *Foreign Policy*, 2 May 2016.

can be noted that these provisions have not yet been used in practice (which does not mean that such a possibility exists).

Finally, there is the law "On the commemoration of the victory over Nazism in the Second World War".[28] The main goal of this regulation is to fight the Russian-centric vision of the war presented in the notion of the "Great Patriotic War" (Rus.: *Великая Отечественная война*). According to the law, the official name of the holiday celebrated on the day of 9 May is the "Day of victory over Nazism in the Second World War". It is the rupture from the name that figured in official documents before 2015, namely "Victory Day" (Ukr.: *День Перемоги*), which, in turn, was a simplified continuation of the official name from the Soviet past – "The holiday of Victory of the Soviet People in the Great Patriotic War of 1941–1945" (Ukr.: *Свято перемоги радянського народу у Великій Вітчизняній війні 1941–1945 рр.*). Along with the introduction of the notion of the Second World War into the calendar of official holidays in Ukraine, the law introduces a new holiday on the day of 8 May – the Day of Remembrance and Reconciliation, thus in line with the UN General Assembly resolution of 22 November 2004, declaring the days of 8–9 May as a time of remembrance and reconciliation.[29]

The UINM, which has regained its role as the key institution in the field of historical justice, has additionally taken steps aimed at building elements of a national identity based on the recent Euromaidan-related events. One of the key ideas in this field is a commemoration of the Euromaidan itself. Voices calling for a need to create a museum devoted to the events of November 2013–February 2014 could be heard almost immediately after the end of the protest. It took, however, almost two years for a new institution, Memorial of Heroes of the Heavenly Hundred – the Museum of the Revolution of Dignity, to be formally registered. The Museum is subordinated to the UINM. At the moment of writing, the Museum exists only as a legal body, according to Igor Poshyvaylo, the director of newly created institution, it is possible to state that the physical creation of the Museum will likely take at least several years.[30] In the meantime, the UINM has initiated several

28 Law of Ukraine 'On commemoration of the victory over Nazism in the Second World War', no. 315-VIII, adopted 9 April 2015.

29 General Assembly of the United Nations, 'Commemoration of the sixtieth anniversary of the end of the Second World War', no. A/RES/59/26, 3 May 2008.

30 Katya Kunitskaya, 'Dyrektor Muzeyu Revolyutsiyi hidnosti: Muzey maye buty komfortnym prostorom, kudy lyudyam zahochetsya pryhodyty i dyskutuvaty', http://culture.lb.ua/news/2016/02/19/328301_direktor_muzeyu_revolyutsii_gidnosti.html (accessed 21 April 2016).

projects aimed at the memorialization of the most recent historic events. One of them titled, "Maidan: an oral history" focuses on collecting video and audio testimonies of activists participating in the protests.[31] Another initiative in this field is the appeal of the UINM to institutions of local self-government to name streets in their towns and villages after soldiers who died during the anti-terrorist operation in the east of the country.[32]

4.4. Effects and challenges

Although we may see some significant connections between the period of Soviet rule and the post-1991 political development of Ukraine, especially in terms of a significant level of continuity within the political elites and presence of communist symbols in the public sphere as well as their constant exploitation for political purposes in independent Ukraine, in practical terms the policy of historical justice is decoupled from the policies of criminal prosecution and vetting. Moreover, historical justice in Ukraine is focused on a completely different period of history, and thus a different stage of transition. From this perspective, the policy is the closest example to the earlier-mentioned concept of "post-transitional justice". Taking into account the lack of a clear public demand for de-communisation and reformulating public memory, one gets the impression that the policy was designed as an afterthought, an additional element to other policies of transitional justice, which responds to the expectations of a group of active proponents of such measures but does not address the urgent needs and expectations of the majority of the Ukrainian society.

As a result, two years after the Euromaidan one can speak rather about a symbolic implementation of the discussed policy signifying a break with the past. The most tangible results have been achieved in the field of changing the topographic names related to the communist legacy. By March 2016, around 400 villages and towns have been renamed.[33] The final round of name changes took

31 The website of the project: http://www.memory.gov.ua/page/maidan-usna-istoriya.

32 Ukrainian Institute of National Memory, 'Instytut natsionalnoyi pam'yati rekomenduye mistam ta selam nazyvaty vulytsi na chest' zahyblyh voyakiv ATO', http://www.memory.gov.ua/news/institut-natsionalnoi-pamyati-rekomendue-mistam-ta-selam-nazvati-vulitsi-na-chest-zagiblikh-voy (accessed 22 April 2016).

33 Ukrayinska Pravda, 'Rada dekomunizuvala Artemivs'k na shche bil'she sta mist i sil', http://www.pravda.com.ua/news/2016/02/4/7097833/ (accessed 20 February 2016); Ukrayinska Pravda, 'Rada dekomunizuvala shche mayzhe 200 sil i mist', http://www.pravda.com.ua/news/2016/03/17/7102444 (accessed 17 March 2016).

place on 19 May 2016, two days before the deadline provided by the law. The total amount of settlements to be renamed is estimated at around 1,000. A survey conducted in September 2015 in Dnipropetrovsk, one of the biggest city falling under the de-communisation law (renamed as Dnipro),[34] has shown that 90.5 percent of respondents preferred not to change the name of city.[35] These data provide the basis for the belief that when faced with the actual renaming of the place in which they live (and thus not answering a question about supporting some abstract idea), people display a significant level of resistance. Such resistance, in turn, may increase political risks for the authorities. Furthermore, the process of de-communisation of names of Ukrainian settlements constitutes an interesting test for the post-Euromaidan judiciary of Ukraine: the question rises as to whether the courts will enforce the implementation of the "de-communisation laws" and punish those responsible for breaking them, should such instances appear. Putting aside the direct goals of de-communisation, the implementation of the regulations adopted in April 2015 itself may be an indicator of the strengthening of the rule of law principle in the country.

It is unfortunately impossible to see measurable effects of the policy of historical justice in terms of change in public attitudes towards both the past and the future in such a short period of time. According to Volodymyr Vyatrovych, the communist and totalitarian legacy is exactly what "prevents the country from development, even if part of its citizens are not aware of it. It does not mean that one should give up de-communisation, it means that one should work hard to make people aware of such a need".[36] Furthermore, Vyatrovych highlights the potential value for democratic development that comes from the process of renaming settlements:

> "In the case of about 900 new names of towns and villages, public debates were held. In some cases, they were held online; in some cases in the circles of expert working groups; in some cases even in the form of assemblies, where citizens are not simply looking for new titles and debate over the old ones. In our opinion, it is the first extensive discussion about values, about what is right and wrong, about crime and punishment, about the

---

34 The city has gained its name in 1926 after the local communist activist Hryhoriy Petrovsky.

35 Kyiv International Institute of Sociology, 'Dumky i pohlyady zhyteliv m. Dnipropetrovska shchodo pereymenuvannya mista: veresen 2015 roku', http://www.kiis.com.ua/?lang=ukr&cat=reports&id=545&page=1 (accessed 22 April 2016).

36 Vyatrovych, supra n 24.

respect to deeds and artistic achievements. Which elements of the heritage of the past are worth preserving and which ones are not?"[37]

The argumentation goes in line with what the literature suggests in terms of the significance of historical justice as an element of wider transitional justice efforts. "Transitional justice is not only played out in the spaces of courtrooms, legislatures and administrations. It is also worked out in public squares, memorial landscapes and museums. [...] These are sites where individual and personal negotiations of transitional justice occur [...]."[38]

An additional challenge to the successful implementation of the policy aimed at a symbolic break with the legacies of the communist past comes from the fact that exactly these values have been utilized by the supporters of separatist movements in Crimea and Donbas. Along with the escalation of the conflict in the east of Ukraine, the state has lost the possibility to control a significant part of its territory. As a result, a large portion of the population, the ones for whom the mentioned Soviet narrative about Ukrainian history remains to be the most convincing, is deprived of the possibility to participate in such "personal negotiations of transitional justice", which in turn may lead to a deepening of existing cleavages. The specific feature of the discussed policy is that despite the fact that is primarily focused on the already distant past, the implementation of it may have a significant impact on the most "future-oriented" dimension of transitional justice in Ukraine – one that deals with the legacy of the Donbas conflict.

37 Ibid.

38 Beattie, supra n 21 at 246–247.

5. Dealing with the legacy of the Donbas conflict

5.1. The essence of the conflict

Almost immediately after the end of the Euromaidan protests, strong centrifugal tendencies were initiated in Ukraine, creating an unprecedented challenge that eventually resulted in armed conflict and consequently in the need to design policies aimed at peacemaking and peacebuilding as well as policies aimed at addressing the consequences of violence and violations of human rights that took place during the conflict. In order to analyse these policies properly a thorough understanding of the roots of the conflict is first required.

On 1 March 2014, the first pro-Russian meetings took place in the cities of Kharkiv, Odesa, Donetsk, Kherson and Mykolaiv. Similar events continued during the spring of 2014 in almost all big cities of eastern and southern Ukraine. The common denominator of these meetings was a disagreement with the change of authorities in Kyiv, which was often referred to as an illegal *coup d'etat*. The image of the Euromaidan protesters as insurgents willing to abolish the legitimate authorities was actively promoted by the Ukrainian government, especially since the beginning of 2014. On 19 February 2014, in the apogee of confrontation, the Security Service of Ukraine initiated an anti-terrorist operation against the protesters, thus suggesting that the latter were nothing but terrorists. This point of view was widely supported in Russian media which had a large audience in Ukraine, in particular—although not exclusively—among Russian-speakers. This interpretation of reality was reinforced after the escape of Viktor Yanukovych from Kyiv. Thanks to the skilful manipulation of facts, a comprehensive narrative was established, opposing the story of the Euromaidan as toppling of a corrupt authoritarian regime by outraged citizens willing to bring their country closer to European political values. In the eyes of the ones dissatisfied with the outcome of the Euromaidan, the winners of the Revolution of Dignity appeared not only as usurpers of power, but also as nationalists or even fascists. Indeed, the Euromaidan gained much greater support in the western *oblasts* of Ukraine. The majority (54.8 percent) of protesters physically present in the Euromaidan camp in the centre of Kyiv were from the western *oblasts* of the country (compared to 23 percent representing central *oblasts* and 21 percent representing eastern and southern *oblasts*).[1] A number of right-wing organisations also penetrated the public awareness due to their active role in the protests (for example, the Right Sector, the most well-known one). In reality, the absolute majority of protesters did not belong to any organisation.[2] At the same time, the results of the later parliamentary elections in October 2014 did not bring any further proof about the growth of popularity of radical right-wing movements and parties in Ukrainian society.

Nevertheless, the mentioned facts were used to revive the Soviet-cherished stereotype of western Ukrainians as Nazi-collaborators[3] and thus use anxiety as one of basic motivations for protests against the post-Euromaidan authorities. In this narrative, Russia appeared as a conservative power able to prevent the assault of unwanted values allegedly promoted by the Euromaidan protesters and the new authorities in Kyiv. In practical terms, the solution was seen as either turning Ukraine into a federal state with significant levels of autonomy for the regions or a separation of the eastern and southern *oblasts* from Ukraine. These were the main slogans of the mass rallies that took place in the east and south of Ukraine in the spring of 2014 (known as the "Russian Spring"), culminating in the annexation of Crimea by Russia and warfare in Donbas.

On the same day of 1 March 2014, the Council of Federation of the Federal Assembly of the Russian Federation adopted a resolution which approved the use of Russian armed forces on the territory of Ukraine. The decision was motivated by the "threat to the life of citizens of the Russian Federation, [their] compatriots, and the personnel of the military contingent of the Armed Forces of the Russian Federation [legally stationing in Crimea]".[4] In retrospect, one can argue that this resolution was issued primarily to legalise the deployment

---

1 Source: Democratic Initiatives Foundation, http://www.dif.org.ua/ua/polls/2014_polls/vid-maidanu-taboru-do-maidan.htm (accessed 25 February 2016).

2 Ibid.

3 The widespread collaboration with Nazi occupants among the inhabitants of today's western Ukraine, as well as of representatives of other Eastern European nations is a complex problem that goes beyond the scope of this analysis. A good analysis of the roots of the problem can be found, among others, in: Timothy Snyder, *Black Earth: The Holocaust as History and Warning* (New York: Tim Duggan Books 2015).

4 Website of the Council of Federation of the Federal Assembly of the Russian Federation, 'Sovyet Fyedyeratsii dal soglasiye na ispol'zovaniye vooruzhennyh sil Rossii na territorii Ukrainy', 01 March 2014, http://council.gov.ru/press-center/news/39851/ (accessed 15 February 2016).

of additional forces[5] in Crimea in order to secure the unconstitutional referendum[6] on independence of Crimea that took place on 16 March 2014. Two days later, on 18 March 2014, the annexation of Crimea was finalized, when an agreement on the joining of the republic of Crimea to the Russian Federation was signed in the Kremlin. The whole process of annexation happened without any resistance from the Ukrainian side and was not accompanied by mass violence.[7]

The most important events from the perspective of this book's analysis took place in the months that followed the annexation of Crimea in the eastern *oblasts* of Donetsk and Luhansk, together making up the Donbas region. The success of the "Crimean operation" inspired the authorities of the Russian Federation to use the anti-Euromaidan sentiments in the east of Ukraine and attempt to repeat the same scenario, with independent "republics", and thus weaken the post-Euromaidan government in Kyiv. Many different analyses speak to the ultimate goal of this strategy, ranging from the disintegration of Ukraine and annexation of the newly-established entities, similar to the Crimean case, to turning Ukraine into a decentralized federation with very limited central power and thus obtaining *de facto* control over the main directions of Ukraine's policy through pro-Russian parts of the federation. It is not the goal here to determine which version was closer to actual reality. What is important from the perspective of this analysis is the outcome of the processes that combined local anti-Euromaidan sentiments and Russian policy towards Ukraine since the beginning of 2014.

During March and April 2014 separatist[8] meetings intensified, with instances of occupation of official buildings throughout the region. On 13 April 2014, the

---

5 Crimea is the base of the Russian Black Sea Fleet, which was stationing there on the basis of the 1997 Treaty on Friendship, Cooperation and Partnership between Ukraine and Russia. Initially, the treaty sanctioned the presence of the fleet till 2017. During the presidency of Viktor Yanukovych, the term was prolonged till 2042.

6 See footnote 34 in chapter 1.

7 The only direct casualty among Ukrainian servicemen was reported to take place on 18 March 2014, during the assault on a military unit: TSN, 'Ukrayins'kyy praporshchyk zahynuv pid chas shturmu viys'kovoyi chastyny u Simferopoli', 18 March 2014, http://tsn.ua/politika/ukrayinskiy-oficer-zaginuv-pid-chas-shturmu-viyskovoyi-chastini-u-simferopoli-340502.html (accessed 15 February 2016). More about the annexation of Crimea: Taras Berezovets, *Aneksiya: ostriv Krym. Hroniky "hibrydnoyi viyny"*, (Kyiv: Brayt Buks, 2015).

8 I am aware of the risks associated with the use of term "separatism", which refers primarily to bottom-up initiative of the population of certain territory to disconnect from the state. As it is presented below, in the case of Donbas it is difficult to talk about a

government of Ukraine approved the beginning of an anti-terrorist operation (ATO) in the east of the country. Since that moment, the "ATO" became an official label used by Ukrainian authorities to describe the events in the east of the country; the territory controlled by separatists and covered by warfare began being referred to as the "ATO zone". Mobilisation of resources and the start of active counter-measures against localized separatism in the eastern parts of Donetsk and Luhansk *oblasts*, helped avoid the "Crimean scenario". Yet, on the other hand, it resulted in an escalation of the conflict into a phase of war by the summer of 2014. On 11 May 2014, unconstitutional referendums took place on the territories captured by the separatists, providing a basis for announcing their independence by the self-proclaimed "people's republics" of Donetsk (DPR) and Luhansk (LPR). Attempts have been taken to negotiate a peaceful resolution of the conflict. The first ceasefire was negotiated in Minsk on 5 September 2014, but failed to last even for several days. The second ceasefire, negotiated on 12 February 2015, appeared to be more effective, but resulted in the lowering of intensity of violence rather than a complete end to it. The relative calmness, although not real peace, was achieved in September 2015.

The separatist ideas have deep roots and existed well before the aftermath of the Euromaidan protests. According to a 2001 census in Ukraine, Russians made up 38.2 percent of the population of the Donetsk *oblast* and 39 percent of the population of the Luhansk *oblast*. This significant ethnic minority was often used as an argument to prove the artificial nature of the Ukrainian state, which allegedly does not respect the interest of this part of the society and even openly discriminates this minority.[9] In reality, if one wants to look for any form of discrimination against the residents of Donbas, it will concern only the sphere of symbols. For example, Marta Studenna-Skrukwa draws attention to the specific kind of moral privilege of western Galicia in the period of the creation of the symbols of newly-established state.[10] At the same time, it is difficult to find any

genuine bottom-up nature of such a movement. However, the term "separatism" seems to have a sufficiently neutral tone and helps avoid even greater risk of taking terminology widely used in the Ukrainian and Russian media (terrorists and insurgents), which in turn may suggest a departure from the principle of objectivity of the research.

9 A prominent example of using this argument can be seen in 2015 documentary by Andrey Kondrashov "Крым. Путь на Родину" (Crimea. A way back to motherland). The movie is published on the official YouTube channel of "Rossiya 24" TV channel: https://youtu.be/t42-71RpRgI.

10 Marta Studenna-Skrukwa, *Ukraiński Donbas. Oblicza tożsamości regionalnej*, (Poznań: Wydawnictwo Nauka i Innowacje, 2014), 273.

concrete evidence to support the thesis about discrimination against Russians or Russian-speakers in post-1991 Ukraine in terms of limitations of economic or language rights. In fact, after Viktor Yanukovych came to power in 2010, the regional elites representing Donbas dominated the central institutions of power in Ukraine.

Steps of separatism have been taken by the local political elites of eastern and southern *oblasts* of Ukraine in the past. During the Orange Revolution, on 28 November 2004, a convention of representatives of local authorities of Luhansk, Mykolaiv, Sumy, Dnepropetrovsk, Donetsk, Poltava, Kherson, Zaporozhe and Odesa *oblasts*, as well as of the Autonomous Republic of Crimea took place in the town of Severodonetsk.[11] A decision was made to hold a referendum on the creation of a South-Eastern Ukrainian Autonomous Republic. The project remained on paper though the convention was rather aimed at expressing support to Viktor Yanukovych at a time when the outcome of the Orange Revolution was still unclear. Nevertheless, it was the first case of open expression of separatist ideas by a part of the political elite of the state. The idea to create such a republic was supported by 34.6 percent of the population of eastern region of Ukraine (the "eastern region" here refers to Kharkiv, Donetsk and Luhansk *oblasts* in the research) and the idea of the hypothetical republic's joining the Russian Federation was supported by 28.6 percent of the population while the idea of its independence by 24.3 percent of the population.[12]

A survey conducted in March 2015 revealed that in the middle of the ongoing conflict, 18.2 percent of the population of Donbas supported the idea of separation of the *oblast* in which they lived from Ukraine and its consequent joining another state (the question did not specify which one exactly). A separation of the whole eastern and southern part of Ukraine and its joining with the Russian Federation was supported by 26.8 percent of inhabitants. Finally, the idea of turning of the *oblast* in which they live into an independent state was supported by 16.6 percent of the population. Interestingly, an absolute majority (89 percent) of inhabitants of Donbas regarded Ukraine as their motherland – a similar result as in the case of the whole country.[13]

---

11 Danylo Yanevsky, *Khronika 'Pomaranchevoyi' revolutsiyi*, (Kharkiv: Folio, 2005), 155.

12 Oleksandr Lytvynenko, 'Ideya pidvyshchennya samostiynosti rehioniv Ukrajiny w konteksti vyborchoyi kampaniyi', *Natsionalna bezpeka i oborona*, no. 11 (2004): 21.

13 Source: Democratic Initiatives Foundation, http://dif.org.ua/ua/polls/2014_polls/dva-misjaci-protestiv-v-ukraini-sho-dali_---zagalnonacionalne-opituvannja.htm (accessed 15 February 2016).

One can thus say that ideas of separatism were supported by a minority of inhabitants of the *oblasts* where active warfare broke out in 2014. At the same time, a minority of 16–25 percent can by no means be regarded as insignificant. The paradoxical dissonance between the level of identification with Ukraine and the support for separatist ideas, along with the fact that the latter appeared in public discourse in previous periods of serious political crisis followed by, at least on the rhetorical level, a turn to pro-European rather than pro-Russian political orientation of new authorities, should be regarded as a manifestation of two different visions of desirable directions of Ukraine's political development. The separatist movements in Ukraine are thus not exclusively manifestations of the denial of the Ukrainian state as such by a part of the society.

"History doesn't know subjunctive mood", reads a popular saying. One cannot say how the situation in Donbas would have developed without the engagement of the Russian Federation. What is clear though is that what has happened is not only the result of spontaneous activity of an active minority promoting separation from Ukraine. There is evidence of Russian support to separatists, which took several forms. Firstly, Russian citizens played leading roles in the organization of both "people's republics" in Donetsk and Luhansk. Igor Girkin/Strelkov, one of military leaders of the DPR, and Aleksandr Borodai, the first "prime minister" of the same "republic" can be mentioned as the most prominent of figures. Evgeny Shibalov, a reporter of the weekly *Zerkalo Nedeli* in the Donetsk *oblast*, calls such persons "paratroopers" – they are usually closely related to Russian security agencies and perform the function of informal representation of Russian interests in decision-making structures of the "republics".[14] Secondly, there is direct military involvement in the "republics", including an open intervention of Russian military forces on the territory of Ukraine in August 2014, when the Kyiv-backed ATO forces started advancing on the separatist forces. This happened without an official declaration of war and Russian officials deny the engagement of their military in the Donbas conflict. The fact was, however, confirmed among others by NATO.[15] Thirdly, Russia played the role as advocate and political protector of the DRP and LPR in the international arena. Additionally, the Russian media

14 Evgeny Shibalov, 'DNR iznutri. Kratkiy likbyez', *Zerkalo Nedeli*, 26 September 2014.

15 On 28 August 2014, presence of the regular Russian armed forces on the territory of Ukraine was confirmed by NATO: North Atlantic Treaty Organisation, 'NATO releases satellite imagery showing Russian combat troops inside Ukraine', 24 August 2014, http://www.nato.int/cps/en/natohq/news_112193.htm?selectedLocale=en (accessed 15 February 2016).

continued spreading the earlier-mentioned narrative of events in Ukraine also in the West.

Before continuing with the analysis of transitional justice mechanisms applied in order to deal with the results of the described conflict, it is necessary to first summarize two important features. First, the essence of the Donbas conflict is defined by the specific contradictions between parts of societies supporting different models of political and socio-economic development: a western-like free market, liberal modernization on the one hand and a state-centred model represented by the Russian Federation on the other. It is in essence a conflict between "modernizationalists" and a specific type of conservatives, willing to preserve the organisation of society they remember from the Soviet past. Finding a compromise between these two groups will inevitably influence the pace of the post-Euromaidan transition in Ukraine. Second, despite being seemingly an internal conflict, its evolution into the phase of war happened due to the involvement of a foreign actor, namely the Russian Federation. From this perspective, dealing with the effects of the conflict will inevitably have international repercussions.

5.2. The scale of violence

Transitional justice mechanisms are usually designed to meet the needs and expectations of the ones affected by large-scale violence. It is therefore important to describe the crimes which define the need to create special policies that will be described below. Here, it is important to stress that the goal of the book is not to judge or place responsibility of any side involved in the conflict for abuses that took place during the war. The only goal of this section is to show the scale and complexity of challenges Ukraine has to face when considering the implementation of such policies.

First and foremost, one should mention mass deaths as a direct result of warfare. According to the United Nations, at least 9,167 people have been killed and 21,044 injured between mid-April 2014 and mid-February 2016.[16] Although the cited report stressed that the average monthly number of casualties after the establishment of relative calmness on the frontlines in September 2015 had been among the lowest since the beginning of the conflict, these numbers should be regarded as indicative ones. Separatist-controlled territories of the DPR and LPR are hardly accessible and thus any kind of thorough assessment regarding the number victims there is difficult. Additionally, the conflict continued bringing

16 United Nations Office of the High Commissioner for Human Rights, 'Report on Human Rights Situation in Ukraine, 16 November 2015 to 15 February 2016', 3 March 2016.

deaths at the moment of writing the book – individual cases of death and injuries among Ukrainian servicemen and civilians have been reported almost every day. Nevertheless, these numbers highlight the scale of the problem – one can expect that a significant part of Ukraine's population have been personally touched by the conflict in some way. It is worth noting that the majority of casualties are civilians – the number of casualties among Ukrainian servicemen was reported to oscillate around 2,000 in August 2014.[17] Once again, it may be hard to assess how the proportion looks like in the case of the self-proclaimed "republics" (not only due to hardships with the accessibility of these territories, but also due to the fact that the legal status of the combatants fighting for the "republics" is unclear). Furthermore, cases of killings took place also outside of the so-called "ATO zone", can thus be regarded as indirect victims of the conflict. The most infamous case is the death of 37 pro-Russian activists in Odesa on 2 May 2014[18] – the result of a confrontation of two meetings: one pro-Ukrainian and one pro-separatist. Another infamous and extremely tragic incident was the downing of the Malaysian jetliner on 17 July 2015, which killed 298 people and drew international attention to the conflict. Along with numerous casualties among the military and civilians, the conflict resulted in mass migration of people inside Ukraine. By the beginning of 2016, there were around 1.6 million internally displaced persons (IDPs) registered by the Ukrainian authorities.[19]

The conflict has inevitably drawn attention of institutions and organisations that deal with problems of human rights violations. Their reports present a more detailed picture of the wrongdoings related with the events in Donbas. One group working for the Polish MP Małgorzata Gosiewska published a catalogue of war crimes committed by the separatists and Russian servicemen, including illegal detention, physical and mental torture, looting and murder.[20] Another report focused on existing proof of human rights violations related to illegal detention

17 Ukrinform, 'Na Donbasi zahynuly ponad dvi tysyachi viys'kovyh – Porohenko', http://www.ukrinform.ua/rubric-iac/1876709-na_donbasi_zaginuli_ponad_dvi_tisyachi_viyskovih___poroshenko_2087291.html (accessed 15 February 2016).

18 Ukrainska Pravda, 'V Odesi bilshe 200 postrazhdalyh, 37 zahyblyh – utochneni dani', 02.05.2014, http://www.pravda.com.ua/news/2014/05/2/7024223/ (accessed 15 February 2016).

19 United Nations, supra n 15.

20 Report 'Rosyjskie zbrodnie wojenne we wschodniej Ukrainie w 2014 roku', http://www.donbasswarcrimes.org/raport/ (accessed 20 February 2016).

on the territories outside the control of the Ukrainian authorities.[21] Despite obvious factual value, such reports have a significant weakness as they focusing solely on the separatist-controlled territories and thus tend to assess the behaviour of only one side of the conflict. Although the central role of Russia in igniting the conflict can hardly be deniable, investigations based on assumptions that only one side of the conflict can commit crimes within the "fog of war" will never be fully objective, even if there is thorough documentation. Furthermore, it is irrelevant from the perspective of international criminal law. Other reports tend to note that cases perpetrated by the widely understood pro-Ukrainian forces,[22] in particular by the volunteer battalions created during the initial phases of the conflict, as response to insignificant capabilities of Ukrainian armed forces and later subordinated to the ministry of interior. Similar information is included in a report by Amnesty International.[23]

Special attention should be paid to Crimea. While the occupation of the peninsula happened without bloodshed, there have been reports that the occupational authorities have initiated oppression against the indigenous Crimean Tatars who, as a majority, does not support the illegal referendum on Crimea's independence. According to Human Rights Watch, "the space for free speech, freedom of association and media in Crimea has shrunk dramatically".[24] However, Ukraine has no possibility to establish any effective policy that would address these wrongdoings directly, focusing primarily on finding possibilities to de-occupy Crimea. Consequently, the problem of Crimea, although being an integral part of the discussed conflict, is not covered in the book.

Summing up, the conflict has produced an extensive number of human rights violations, as well as challenges for the Ukrainian state to comply with existing obligations in the field of human rights. Along with the most obvious violations of the right to live, the right to liberty, security and physical integrity, it brought significant challenges in the field of economic and social rights.

---

21 Iurii L. Bielousov et al., *Surviving Hell: Testimonies of Victims on Places of Illegal Detention in Donbas*, (Kyiv: TsP Komprint, 2015).

22 The International Federation for Human Rights, *Eastern Ukraine. Civilians caught in the crossfire*, October 2015, no. 667a, 21–24.

23 Amnesty International Report 2015/16, *The State of the World's Human Rights*, 378–382.

24 Human Rights Watch, 'Ukraine: Fear, Repression in Crimea. Rapid Rights Deterioration in 2 Years of Russian Rule', 18 March 2016, https://www.hrw.org/news/2016/03/18/ukraine-fear-repression-crimea (accessed 20 March 2016).

5.3. Theoretical background: transitional justice in an ongoing conflict

As it was mentioned in the introductory chapter, there is an inevitable tension that exists between maintaining peace and delivering justice. This tension predictably raises the policy dilemma in any transition of political regimes: "The incoming forces often have two conflicting desires: for a peaceful transition and for transitional justice."[25] The problem is even more obvious in the case of an open military conflict when the question is not how to avoid violence, but how to stop it along with how to bring peace and stabilize it by minimizing the social tensions caused by impunity of the ones responsible for abuses during the conflict. On the one hand, the threat of criminal accountability may deter future abuses. One can also expect that offenders may regard the risk of facing such accountability as an additional motivation in order to prolong the active phase of the conflict, thus leading to more abuses. As Jemima Garcia-Godos and Chandra Lekha Sriram note, the question is not "*whether* accountability is possible in the process of peacemaking and peacebuilding, but whether and, if so, *how* greater integration between the two might be achieved."[26]

The tension between peacemaking and transitional justice is obvious especially in the short-term perspective, when the priority is given to an effective disarmament, demobilization and reintegration (DDR) policy – a set of mechanisms targeted primarily at combatants, aimed at convincing them to return to "normal life". As Lars Waldorf notes, the reintegration element of such policies is exactly the field where transitional justice mechanisms have the biggest potential to contribute to settlement of the long-lasting peace, due to the obvious economic, social and political dimensions of the former.[27] Thus, at the stage of reintegration there is much larger potential to involve different approaches to ensure that wrongdoers will not have motivation to return to an active phase of conflict. The same conclusion can be drawn from the literature on conflict theory which points to the distinction between "negative" and "positive" peace. The former

---

25 Jon Elster, *Closing the Books. Transitional Justice in Historical Perspective*, (Cambridge: Cambridge University Press, 2004), 190.

26 Jemima Garcia-Godos and Chandra Lekha Sriram, 'Introduction', in *Transitional Justice and Peacebuilding on the Ground. Victims and ex-combatants*, ed. Chandra Lekha Sriram et al., (London and New York: Routledge, 2013), 4.

27 Lars Waldorf, 'Just peace? Integrating DDR and transitional justice', in *Transitional Justice and Peacebuilding on the Ground. Victims and ex-combatants*, ed. Chandra Lekha Sriram et al., (London and New York: Routledge, 2013), 65.

refers to secession of direct violence; in order to achieve the latter, injustice must be removed.[28] If one looks from this perspective, transitional justice mechanisms may appear as an important condition to reach the stage of long-lasting positive peace. In other words, one should expect that a comprehensive transitional justice policy would be introduced only after disarmament and demobilisation of combatants. It also means that the political consensus between the sides of the conflict that leads to disarmament and demobilisation may contain provisions that will constrain the transitional justice mechanisms. Some types of wrongdoings cannot be a matter of compromise, however. In particular, this refers to international crimes that fall under a universal jurisdiction.

All conflicts are unique. Along with the general constraints for implementing transitional justice mechanisms as a response to wrongdoings produced by an armed conflict as suggested by the existing literature, one should also pay attention to the specific conditions of the case. In the Donbas conflict, there is one element that will have a strong impact in the application of transitional justice mechanisms – the strong international component of the conflict (or, as some might argue, the very essence of the conflict is international). The annexation of Crimea which ignited the conflict, the concealed, and officially denied, support of Russia for separatist forces in Donbas means that a consensus to solve the conflict is hardly achievable without Russia's involvement (and other international actors) in the peace negotiations. As a result, the design and implementation of transitional justice policies in the discussed case is constrained by problems typical for the domain of international relations: sovereignty, balance of power, and a lack of authority able to induce implementation of achieved agreements. At the same time, the nature of abuses paves the way to an application of the framework of international criminal justice, which is not transitional justice in a narrow sense but can undoubtedly be supplementary; in particular, it may have an impact on the course of prosecutions. Ultimately, the conflict may fit into the trend of judicial intervention in the midst of a conflict[29] and thus create the possibility for an assessment of international criminal justice on the peacemaking and peacebuilding process.

Thus, the theory suggests that in the long run, transitional justice, in a narrow sense, may play a significant role in achieving long-lasting peace and reconciliation.

---

28 Oliver Ramsbotham, Tom Woodhouse and Hugh Miall, *Contemporary conflict resolution: the prevention, management and transformation of deadly conflicts*, 3rd ed. (Cambridge, Malden: Polity Press, 2011), 11–12.

29 See: Par Engstrom, 'Transitional Justice and Ongoing Conflict', in *Transitional Justice and Peacebuilding on the Ground. Victims and ex-combatants*, ed. Chandra Lekha Sriram et al., (London and New York: Routledge, 2013).

Even though the conflict is still ongoing, peacemaking and peacebuilding efforts create a basis and a framework for implementing future transitional justice mechanisms. In the particular case of the Donbas conflict, these efforts are influenced first of all by the position of international actors involved in the peace negotiations, especially Russia. Last but not least, politicians are inevitably interested in maximising their electoral chances and thus expectations of the society towards the discussed issue cannot be ignored, including the ones that gave the legitimacy to the post-Euromaidan authorities.

5.4. Peace process: establishment of framework for the future transitional justice policies

It is not the purpose of this chapter to analyse the process of the peace negotiations in Ukraine. Instead, the focus is on how the agreements achieved at different stages of the conflict refer to the problem of transitional justice. Peace talks referring to the situation in Ukraine began already at the early stages of escalation of the conflict. On 17 April 2014, representatives of the Ukrainian government, the European Union, the United States and Russia concluded an agreement in Geneva with the main aim to deescalate growing tensions and provide security. The agreement included four main points: (1) prevention of violence and provocations by all sides; (2) a disarmament of all illegal armed groups and release of illegally seized buildings and public offices; (3) amnesty for all protestors who agree to leave seized buildings and surrender weapons, with the exceptions of those found guilty of capital crimes; and (4) an inclusive constitutional process to be carried out through a broad national dialogue.[30] As was illustrated earlier, the agreement was ineffective. The escalation continued, and the months following the Geneva talks witnessed the most violent acts of the war in the east of Ukraine.

In June 2014, the Trilateral Contact Group was created, including representatives of Ukraine, Russia and the Organisation for Security and Cooperation in Europe (OSCE) aimed at facilitating a diplomatic resolution of the conflict. The group drafted the agreement that was signed on 5 September 2014 in Minsk by the representatives of the OSCE, Ukraine (former president Leonid Kuchma), Russia (Russian ambassador to Ukraine Mikhail Zurabov) and leaders of self-proclaimed "republics" of DPR and LPR (Alexander Zakharchenko and Igor Plotnitskiy).

---

30 Zerkalo Nedeli, 'Povnyy tekst zayavy za pidsumkamy perehovoriv u Zhenevi z ukrayins'koho pytannya', 17 April 2014, http://dt.ua/POLITICS/povniy-tekst-zayavi-za-pidsumkami-peregovoriv-u-zhenevi-z-ukrayinskogo-pitannya-141885_.html (accessed 20 February 2016).

The so-called Minsk-1 protocol contained the following points: (1) an immediate bilateral ceasefire; (2) establishment of a monitoring and verification regime of the ceasefire to be carried out by the OSCE; (3) a decentralisation of powers in Ukraine, including the introduction of a special regime of self-governance in the districts occupied by the DPR and LPR forces; (4) a permanent monitoring of the Ukrainian-Russian border and verification by the OSCE; (5) an immediate release of all hostages and illegally detained persons; (6) amnesty for DPR and LPR combatants; (7) a continuation of an inclusive national dialogue; (8) measures to improve the humanitarian situation in Donbas; (9) early local elections in accordance with the law introducing the special regime of self-governance in the districts controlled by DPR and LPR forces; (10) a withdrawal of illegally-armed groups and military equipment as well as fighters and mercenaries from Ukraine; (11) the adoption of a program of economic recovery and reconstruction for the Donbas region; (12) personal security for participants of the consultations.[31] Once again the agreement appeared to have been ineffective.

Peace negotiations continued and included more international actors, in particular France and Germany, whose leaders, together with presidents Petro Poroshenko of Ukraine and Vladimir Putin of Russia formed the so-called Normandy Format of diplomatic talks over the situation in Ukraine. On 11 February 2015, a summit took place in Minsk, Belarus attended by Vladimir Putin, Petro Poroshenko, German Chancellor Angela Merkel, and French President François Hollande. The DPR and LPR leaders, Alexander Zakharchenko and Igor Plotnitskiy also took part in the talks. As a result of the negotiations, a new protocol was signed on 12 February 2015, widely referred to as the Minks-2 protocol. In fact, it was not a new agreement, but contained a roadmap to implement the agreement achieved in September 2014. The Minsk-2 protocol was signed by the same representatives as the Minsk-1. The provisions of the second Minsk protocol included: (1) an immediate and full ceasefire; (2) a pull-out of all heavy weapons by both sides; (3) monitoring and verification of the implementation of points 1 and 2 by the OSCE; (4) a start of dialogue on modalities of conducting local elections in the rebel-controlled territories in accordance with Ukrainian law; (5) amnesty; (6) the release and exchange of all hostages and illegally held persons; (7) access to humanitarian aid by the ones in need; (8) dialogue on the modalities of a full restoration of social and economic connections between the separatist-controlled

31 The text of the Minsk-1 protocol is retrieved from the website of the Organisation for Security and Co-operation in Europe: http://www.osce.org/ru/home/123258?download=true (accessed 23 February 2016).

territories and the rest of Ukraine; (9) restoration of control by Ukraine over the state border; (10) a withdrawal of all foreign armed formations, military equipment, and also mercenaries groups from the territory of Ukraine; (11) local elections in the territories controlled by the "people's republics"; (12) an intensification of the work of the Trilateral Contact Group.[32] These provisions were agreed to be implemented by the end of 2015, which was later extended into 2016.

Assuming that the described Minsk process – despite all its disadvantages proved by the challenge of their implementation – will remain the basic framework for the peacemaking and peacebuilding process, one can analyse its possible impact on the design of transitional justice policies addressing the wrongdoings that took place during the conflict.

The logic of the Minsk process is obviously not aimed primarily at accountability but at the stopping violence and to commence the process of disarmament and demilitarization. Referring to the earlier-mentioned policy dilemma between peace and justice, the preferences are granted to the former. From Geneva to Minsk-2, two components have been continuously emphasised. The first is a "national dialogue" which should lead to an unspecified transformation of the political system of Ukraine, the basic goal of which is the introduction of autonomy for the rebellious territories. The second is "amnesty", which should basically provide protection from criminal prosecution to the combatants, collaborators and supporters of the "people's republics". The most direct interpretation of this logic be as follows: let us leave everything as it is and focus on the future; let us try to find a new political and social order based on a consensus that will help avoid discrimination of any part of the society.

Such logic could be successful should the conflict have exclusively internal roots and both sides of it would genuinely long for reconciliation. In this case, however, the actors directly engaged in the Minsk process regard the end of violence as instrumental for achieving other goals. These goals can be interpreted as following. The West (as represented in the process by France and Germany) is interested primarily in stabilizing the situation without considering the political costs for Ukraine. This would in part allow greater focus on much more urgent problems facing the European Union including the refugee crisis and the risk of disintegration of the EU. On the contrary, Russia and the self-proclaimed "people's republics" (which in this case can be regarded as one party due to the

32 The text of the Minsk-2 protocol is retrieved from the website of the Organisation for Security and Co-operation in Europe: http://www.osce.org/cio/140156 (accessed 23 February 2016).

political patronage of Moscow over Donetsk and Luhansk as discussed above) are interested in the destabilisation of the political situation in Ukraine. This would allow the "republics" to gain ground and provide Russia with a new frozen conflict, a well-studied tool of exerting influence on policies of post-Soviet countries. In this triangle, only Ukraine is interested in finding a long-lasting consensus that would serve as an additional foundation for the post-Euromaidan political order, which is still in the process of being built. Hence, one should not expect that the seemingly easy logic of transitional justice foreseen by the Minsk protocols will eventually be implemented. It becomes obvious when one looks at how the sides of the conflict set their accents on which point of agreements is actually the most important one. From the perspective of the Russian side, changes in Ukrainian legislation, including amnesty, is often presented as a primary step.[33] Ukrainian authorities, in turn, underline that without definitive stop of violence and demilitarisation no other step can be effectively implemented.[34]

Therefore, implementation of criminal accountability to the ones responsible for wrongdoings taking place during the Donbas conflict as well as a comprehensive approach to amnesties remain largely dependent on the course of negotiations referring to peacemaking and peacebuilding. At the same time, this dependence is not absolute: evidently, the Ukrainian authorities support the policy of amnesty in their negotiations with other sides of the conflict. One should also remember that the obligation to implement amnesty is not absolute, taking into account that in accordance to international law, there can be no guaranty of immunity for those responsible for the so-called international crimes, as it was already mentioned in chapter 2. Furthermore, similar to other cases of implementation of transitional justice policies, the policy supply remains dependent on social expectations regarding peace and justice.

5.5. Demand: social expectations regarding peace and justice

In the perception of Ukrainian citizens, the Donbas conflict has become the most significant political problem of Ukraine, overshadowing even the serious problem

33 See footnote 27 in chapter 6.

34 For example: Statement of the President of Ukraine H.E. Petro Poroshenko at the 13th Yalta European Strategy Annual Meeting (YES) "The World, Europe and Ukraine: storms of changes", available on the website of the President of Ukraine: http://www.president.gov.ua/en/news/vistup-prezidenta-petra-poroshenka-na-13-j-shorichnij-zustri-38163 (accessed 22 September 2016).

of corruption[35] – one of fundamental reasons for the mass protests at the end of 2013-beginning of 2014. Assuming that the politicians are inevitably interested in increasing their share of electorate, one should expect that public attitudes towards the conflict and the ways of its resolution will be taken into account, and thus influence the design of transitional justice mechanisms. Since the beginning of the ATO by the Ukrainian authorities, several surveys have been conducted, the results of which allow us to create a more or less comprehensive picture reflecting public attitudes towards this problem.

The most basic issue is how Ukrainians perceive the nature of the Donbas conflict. The absolute majority of Ukrainians agree with the statement that the conflict is in fact an aggressive war of Russia against Ukraine (50.1 percent in August 2015, which is a decline from 56.1 percent declared in March 2015). On the other side, the clear minority consider it to be a civil conflict (13.6 percent in August 2015, 15.6 percent in March 2015). What is interesting, a significant group of respondents tend to look for more sophisticated explanations, namely that the conflict is in essence a struggle between the United States and Russia over a sphere of influence (25.9 percent in August 2015; 18.6 percent in March 2015).[36] The same research revealed much more confidence regarding the essence of the self-proclaimed "people's republics". In August 2015, 64.9 percent of Ukrainians stated that the DPR and LPR are terrorist organisations that have no right to represent the population of the territories they control, thus agreeing with the official narrative of the Ukrainian authorities. At the same time, only 16.3 percent agreed that both organisations are representatives of that part of the population. Significantly, almost one-fifth of respondents (18.7 percent) had no opinion on the matter.[37] The presented data can serve as proof that the majority of Ukrainians generally understand the essence of the ongoing conflict. Despite the fact that martial law was not introduced, Ukrainians generally see the conflict as a *de facto* war, in which Russia is engaged. One should also pay attention to the minorities that perceive the conflict as an internal one and the rebellious "republics" as legitimate representatives of some portion of citizens. This illustrates that this portion of the public opinion can also assume that the responsibility for the

---

35 Source: International Republican Institute, http://www.iri.org/resource/iri%E2%80%99s-center-insights-poll-pessimism-high-after-two-years-violent-conflict-russia-people (accessed 17 January 2016).

36 Source: Razumkov Centre, http://www.razumkov.org.ua/ukr/poll.php?poll_id=1026 (accessed 20 January 2016).

37 Source: Razumkov Centre, http://www.razumkov.org.ua/ukr/poll.php?poll_id=1025 (accessed 20 January 2016).

wrongdoing taking place during the conflict lays (at least partially) on the side of the Ukrainian authorities.

When speaking about how to resolve the conflict, the image is even less clear. According to a survey conducted by the Razumkov Centre in August 2015, the continuation of the ATO until the moment of restoration of control over the separatist-controlled territories was the most preferable option (34.4 percent in August 2015). In addition, 19.9 percent of respondents supported the idea of separation of the DPR and LPR from Ukraine, while 28.5 percent preferred providing the territories with a special status within Ukraine.[38] The series of alternative surveys by the Democratic Initiatives Foundation illustrate an even more nuanced picture. Figure 6 presents the preferable options of the conflict resolution divided by macro regions.

Figure 6: Ukraine's public opinion towards the acceptability of compromises for the sake of achieving peace in Donbas (September 2014)[39]

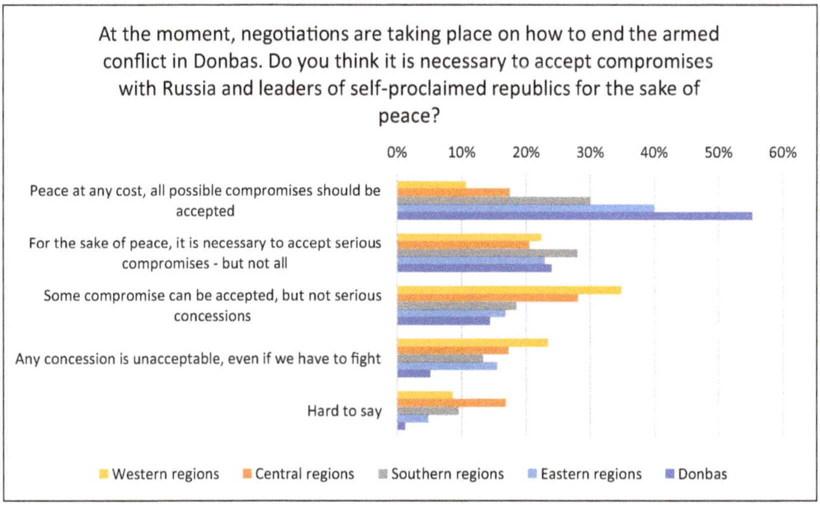

Source: Democratic Initiatives Foundation, http://dif.org.ua/ua/polls/2014_polls/stavlenne-opitu-vannja.htm (accessed 20 January 2016).

38 Source: Razumkov Centre, http://www.razumkov.org.ua/ukr/poll.php?poll_id=1028 (accessed 20 January 2016).

39 The survey hasn't covered the territories occupied by DPR and LPR as well as the territory of annexed Crimea.

The survey was conducted several days after the Minsk-1 protocol was signed. One year later, a similar survey was conducted. In this case, the number of answer options was reduced, thus making a direct comparison of the two periods difficult (Figure 7). Nevertheless, one can draw some conclusions regarding the dynamics of public attitudes towards the acceptability of compromises as a means to resolve the conflict.

Figure 7: Ukraine's public opinion toward the acceptability of compromises for the sake of achieving peace in Donbas (October 2015)

Source: Democratic Initiatives Foundation, http://www.dif.org.ua/ua/publications/press-relizy/stavlennja-nasnfliktu.htm (accessed 20 January 2016).

The majority of Ukrainians express interest in achieving peace, and state that they are ready to accept concessions provided to the combatants of the DPR and LPR and their political patrons. Furthermore, the number of this group tends to grow as the conflict perpetuates. What is even more interesting is that there is an obvious regional disproportion in the level of acceptance of compromise. Generally speaking, the farther respondents are from the conflict area the more uncompromising position they tend to have; for those living in the direct vicinity of the self-proclaimed "republics" (and thus the ones who have most likely witnessed or experienced the war personally), the undisputable priority is the end of warfare at all possible costs.

The question of public attitudes and expectations regarding the post-conflict justice and accountability is much harder to answer unequivocally, in particular due to the lack of surveys covering this matters in a clear manner. However, the mentioned survey by the Democratic Initiatives Foundation contained an important question on what – according to respondents – should be done in order to achieve peace in Donbas. The results are presented in Figure 8.

Figure 8: The perception by Ukrainians of steps necessary to achieve peace in Donbas (October 2015)[40]

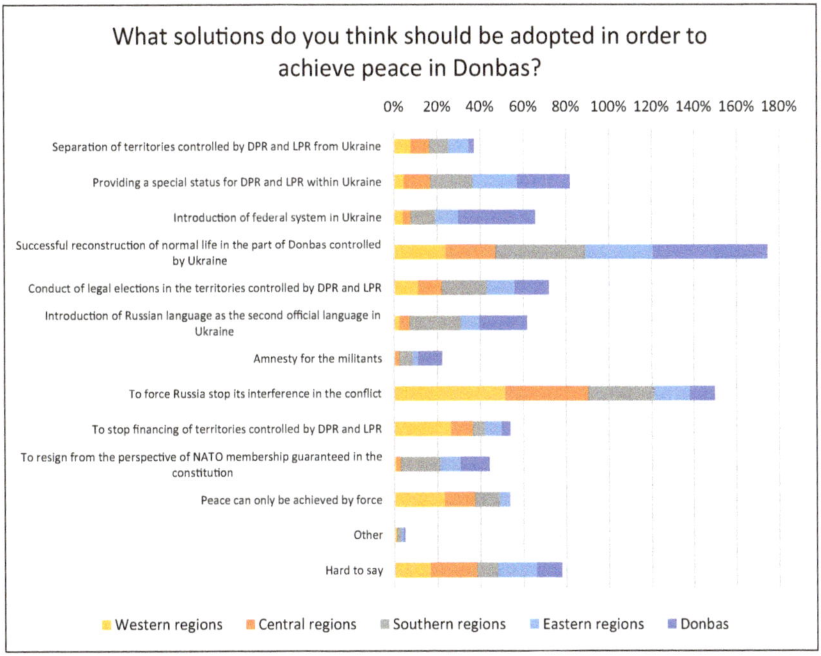

Source: Democratic Initiatives Foundation, http://www.dif.org.ua/ua/publications/press-relizy/stavlennja-nasnfliktu.htm (accessed 20 January 2016).

40 The respondents had a possibility to choose three answers, therefore the sum of percentages in each row may exceed one hundred. The size of rows shows the general perception of importance of a given issue.

The picture generally corresponds with the abovementioned perception of the nature of the conflict. Three conditions dominate the picture: forcing Russia to withdraw from the conflict; a restoration of "normal life" in the part of Donbas controlled by Ukraine (assuming that it may become a sort of "soft power" that will help not only end the war, but also reintegrate the occupied territories in the future); providing DPR and LPR with a special status. The only issue that refers directly to transitional justice in a narrow meaning (amnesty) is regarded as the least important. This is natural in the context of a clear prioritization in stopping the violence. There are reasons to think that after the desired peace is achieved, the demand to deal with the aftermath of mass wrongdoings accompanying the conflict will rise.

Figure 9: Perception of conflicts by the residents of parts of Donetsk and Luhansk oblasts controlled by Ukraine (February 2015)

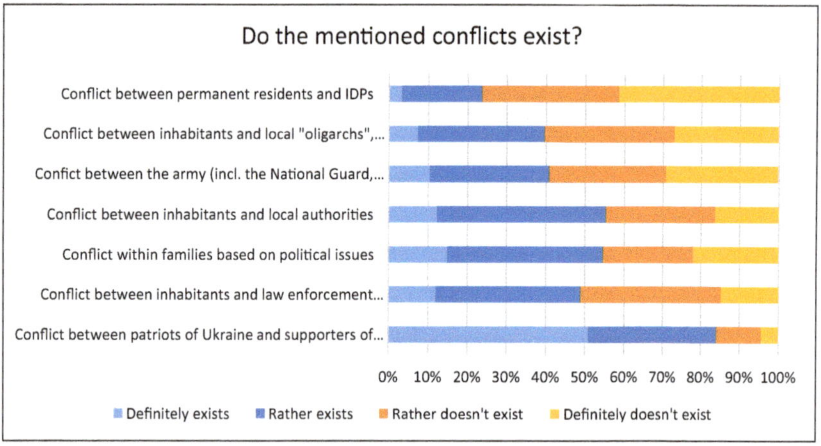

Source: Information Centre "Maidan Monitoring", http://maidan.org.ua/2015/03/nasha-sotsiolohiya-transformatsiya-sotsialno-politychnyh-uyavlen-ta-visi-konfliktiv-v-zoni-ato/ (accessed 22 January 2016).

The data presented in Figure 9 reflect the social tensions perceived by the Ukrainian citizens residing in the direct vicinity of the conflict area. Once again, there is a clear confidence about existence of conflict between "pro-Ukrainians" and "pro-separatists", a significant amount of people convinced about the existing conflicts between the local population on the one hand and local authorities, law enforcement agencies, armed formations and even businesses on the other hand can be interpreted as a result of the experience of some form of unjust action from their side in the conditions of a *de facto* war taking place in that area. It is impossible to say definitively as to what extent this is a reflection of an objective reality versus a subjective perception of it. Nevertheless, the issue cannot be ignored as such perception can be translated into a political demand to deal with the (alleged or real) problem. This in turn could drive the political supply resulting in policies addressing the presented conflicts.

In conclusion, there is a clear demand from the side of the Ukrainian citizens to stop the ongoing conflict. Most of them are ready to accept some level of concession, although the scope of concessions differs depending on the region. In addition, one can conclude that Ukrainians tend to accept the idea of a new constitutional compromise that would provide the self-proclaimed "republics" with political privileges, while the overwhelming majority supports the unity of Ukraine. While on average the position of Ukrainian citizens is rather moderate, extreme solutions (peace at all cost or war till the victorious end) are not the most popular, the Ukrainian authorities will obviously face the problem of regional disparities in the acceptable scope of compromise. In other words, it is hard to imagine a compromise that would be accepted by the overwhelming majority of Ukrainians as the most optimal solution. Furthermore, although the issue of accountability for wrongdoings accompanying the conflict seems not to be in the focus of public opinion at the moment, one can assume that the importance of accountability will rise as soon as peace is achieved and existing social tensions will overwhelm popular expectations to stop violence.

5.6. Supply: prosecutions, amnesties and involvement of the ICC

Prosecutions are clearly the most visible and at the same time the most measurable way to bring to justice to those responsible for crimes committed during an armed conflict. Just as in the case of the post-Euromaidan investigations and trials (discussed in chapter 2), one should remember that Ukraine's penal system is based on the *nullum crimen sine lege* principle. Thus, what should be noted at the very beginning is the fact that the criminal code of Ukraine does not contain a crime described as separatism. Therefore, in order to deal with the multi-dimensional problem which is referred to in this book as separatism, the Ukrainian authorities have used other provisions of the criminal code. These can generally be distinguished as two types. The first falls into the category of crimes against state security, in particular, "encroachment on the territorial integrity and inviolability", as defined in the criminal code of Ukraine. The second category is made up of crimes committed during the conflict itself.

Ukraine's policies in this field are strongly constrained by the legal definition of the conflict. Although there is a legal basis to speak about Russia's aggression against Ukraine at least since the beginning of the occupation of Crimea,[41] and the notion of "war" is constantly used in the Ukrainian public debate since the spring of 2014, including by the highest officials, the country is formally not in a state of war. The logic behind not introducing martial law is clearly reflected in the transcript of the meeting of the National Security and Defence Council (NSDC)[42] which took place on 28 February 2014. Along with an extremely underprepared army, the primary concern of Ukrainian decision-makers was that an introduction of martial law would support the Russian narrative of a "military junta" taking power in Kyiv in the aftermath of the Euromaidan and thus serve as a justification for a massive intervention of Russian armed forces. Additionally, western partners advised the Ukrainian government to refrain itself from such actions, also in fear of greater intervention in Ukraine from the side of Russia.[43] As a result, the Ukrainian response became the aforementioned anti-terrorist operation. This, in turn may have an influence on the legal interpretations of incidents of violence as well as identification of the ones responsible for them and bringing them to justice.

There are only several indicators that can provide us with information about the effectiveness of the prosecutions of crimes against state sovereignty. In an interview given to *Fakty* newspaper on 17 October 2015, the General Prosecutor of Ukraine Viktor Shokin stated that about 500 cases of "separatism and terrorism" had been submitted in the courts. However, at the time of writing, it was unclear how many people would be ultimately punished as well as what are the actual legal interpretations of these acts (having in mind that there is no such crime as "separatism") and whether the acts committed are indeed recognised as terrorism. Additionally, cooperation with foreign intelligence services, acting against national security and territorial integrity of Ukraine, public calls

---

41 See: Ireneusz C. Kamiński, 'International Law Aspects of the Situation in Ukraine', in *The Maidan Uprising, Separatism and Foreign Intervention. Ukraine's Complex transition*, ed. Klaus Bachmann and Igor Lyubashenko (Frankfurt am Main: Peter Lang Edition, 2014).

42 The National Security and Defence Council is the institution headed by the president of Ukraine, which coordinates and controls activities of the executive in the field of national security and defence.

43 The document is retrieved from the website of the Committee for National Security and Defence of the Verkhovna Rada of Ukraine: http://komnbo.rada.gov.ua/komnbo/control/uk/publish/article?art_id=53495&cat_id=44731 (accessed 26 February 2016).

for violation of territorial integrity and sovereignty of Ukraine, and fomenting ethnic strife have been defined as one of the lustrable offences according to the lustration law adopted on 16 September 2014.[44] Although the formulations are quite vague, in a given context this regulation is undoubtedly designed to apply the logic of administrative justice against state officials involved in separatism. There is no information regarding how many have been lustrated on the basis of this particular provision. What is clear, however, is that unlike the "classic" lustrable offences (i.e. being an element of state apparatus of the *ancien regime*), this is focused on a much more ordinary crime, which means that guilt should be proved in court for each particular case. Administrative justice in this case is thus strongly dependent on effectiveness of criminal prosecutions.

Addressing the crimes against state security turned out to be a difficult task. On the one hand, it seems far from being controversial. The crimes of encroachment on the territorial integrity and inviolability have been defined by the criminal code long before the outbreak of the conflict and punishment of such acts has no retrospective nature. On the other hand, in a given situation the problem has gained clear political significance. When there are centrifugal processes taking place in the country, including a third powerful party which clearly supports the ones calling for encroachment of the country's territorial integrity, even if they are in a minority, state officials who risk being prosecuted can easily turn against the central government. The case of *Berkut* special police units running away to occupied Crimea exemplifies this case (although these officers faced charges other than undermining state security). Another example is demonstrated by the Ukrainian soldiers stationed in Crimea who quickly turned to the Russian side during the annexation. This is similar to the earlier-mentioned case of the unsuccessful attempt to create a South-Eastern Ukrainian Autonomous Republic in 2004. As then and as well as in 2014, actions bearing signs of encroachment on the territorial integrity and inviolability taken by politicians and officials can be seen as a result of calculation and assessment of the situation in a given moment of time considering the odds of whether the new interim government will survive, whether Ukraine will maintain its integrity, or whether the "Russian Spring" will lead to creation of a new state. Thus, making a determination to support the uncertain new government or refuse to obey it.

The answers to these and many other questions were far from obvious in the spring of 2014. While by no means should it be regarded as a justification of the side of the unrecognised "people's republics" or a lack of professionalism in those

44 See chapter 3 to learn more about vetting in post-Euromaidan Ukraine.

performing a public service, these considerations illustrate that not all manifestations of support to the "authorities" of the DPR and LPR, especially in the initial phases of the conflict, are driven by genuine beliefs. In 2004, the state did not punish anyone for a clear act of encroachment on the territorial integrity, thus creating a dangerous precedence. In 2014, the political position of the interim government was much weaker, hence the obvious political calculation not to push for mass prosecutions of alleged "separatists" and collaborators among politicians and state officials.

The prosecution of crimes committed in the course of the conflict is undoubtedly a challenging task as well. And it is also associated with significant political risks. The General Prosecutor of Ukraine has begun a number of investigations following the most brutal cases of shelling of civilian objects and killings of Ukrainian servicemen. According to the above-mentioned logic, these incidents are qualified as terrorist attacks. A separate investigation of the Odesa incident is also ongoing. Generally speaking, according to available statistics, as many as 2,088 crimes that fall into the category of terrorism have been registered in Ukraine in 2014, and 1,717 of such crimes registered in the period between January and July 2015. What draws special attention, however, is the drastically smaller amount of people convicted of these crimes during this same time period: a total of nine.[45] This is partially explained by the objective inability to execute law on the territories under the control of the self-proclaimed "republics". There is also grounds to argue about the insufficient capacity of the Ukrainian state to conduct good-quality investigations and thus make steps towards punishing the guilty. One of the most significant findings come from a comprehensive report prepared by the FIDH, which states that the Ukrainian authorities are unable "to investigate and prevent the serious crimes committed by the countries' own armed forces and volunteers, as well as violations by actors on the so-called LPR/DPR side".[46] While this inability may be understandable in the conditions of the ongoing conflict, the insufficient capacity to investigate the Odesa incident reported by the Council of Europe[47] is a more worrisome indicator. Official reports can only be supplemented by observations of journalists covering the cases of ignoring crimes committed by

---

45 Zerkalo Nedeli, 'Za posledniye poltora goda v Ukrainye za terrorizm osudili vsego devyat chelovek', 28 November 2015, http://zn.ua/UKRAINE/za-poslednie-poltora-goda-v-ukraine-za-terrorizm-osudili-vsego-devyat-chelovek-196808_.html (accesses 20 February 2016).

46 The International Federation for Human Rights, supra n 22 at 5.

47 International Advisory Panel, 'Report of the International Advisory Panel on its Review of the Maidan Investigations', 31 March 2015.

the DPR and LPR combatants by local law enforcement agencies on the territories released from the "republics".[48] A comprehensive analysis of Ukraine's approach to criminal prosecution of the ones engaged in the Donbas conflict would require additional research based on studying the materials of individual cases. What is important, however, is that when analysing the Ukrainian public debate, one can easily find opinions that such instances can be explained by "deals" between the local elites (public officials at different levels, business etc.) and the ones who committed some kind of wrongdoing. In other words, such instances are regarded as manifestations of a similar calculation (such was the case of the prosecution of crimes against the state sovereignty), but in a much smaller local context: "Does it pay off to prosecute someone whom I know personally, if I am not sure whether he/she has actually done something wrong, but who was probably forced to follow the separatists when everything was so unclear and unstable?" It is thus less important as to whether such "deals" actually exist and what their scale is. When such stories make their way into the public debate and contribute to the general pessimistic mood and conviction that even such events as *de facto* war does not change the actual attitude of the state to obliging law.

Indeed, it is very challenging to determine personal responsibility in each individual case during an armed conflict and/or in conditions of loss of sovereignty over a part of a state's territory. Therefore, amnesty can be regarded as a legitimate form of justice addressed at common combatants engaged in the conflict. As was mentioned above, the conflict in Donbas is not an exception: amnesty was even included in both Minsk agreements. At the time of writing the book, no special law regulating the rules of amnesty for the combatants fighting for DPR/LPR was adopted, although there were attempts to do so. On 16 September 2014, a law "On special order of local self-government in certain areas of Donetsk and Luhansk oblasts" (the term used to call territories controlled by the self-proclaimed "people's republics") was adopted in order to start implementing the agreement achieved in Minsk several days earlier. The law will be discussed in more details in chapter 6; what should be stressed here is that article 3 of the law guarantees avoidance of prosecution, criminal and administrative responsibility and punishment of persons involved in the "events in the territory of Donetsk and Luhansk *oblasts*". However, this *de facto* amnesty hasn't entered into force because it was conditioned by prior conduct of local elections in accordance with Ukrainian law.

48 Mariya Tomak, 'Zwilneni terytoriyi Donbasu: pravoohorontsi ignoruyut' zlochyny boyovykiv?', 03 October 2015, http://www.radiosvoboda.mobi/a/27256092.html (accessed 19 February 2016).

Furthermore, on the same day of 16 September 2014, President Poroshenko submitted to the parliament a draft law "On avoiding prosecution and punishment of those participating in the events in Donetsk and Luhansk oblasts"[49] that would pave the way to close criminal prosecution of combatants who haven't committed serious crimes. This law, however, was not adopted.

The main stumbling block for the introduction of amnesty should be sought in the various ways of interpreting the Minsk agreements. While the separatists, as well as Russia, demand amnesty as one of the initial steps in the peacemaking process, the Ukrainian authorities expect amnesty to pre-conditioned on the fulfilment of the first points of the agreement. Despite the lack of a comprehensive solution to the problem of amnesty, the Ukrainian government has initiated a program which would allow former militants (who haven't committed felonies and expressed a willingness to cooperate with the authorities) to "reintegrate" back into society. The scale of this program is rather small, covering only 60 people between August 2015 and January 2016,[50] suggesting that such efforts will probably not have a significant impact on the course of the peace negotiations.

At the same time, steps were taken to grant amnesty to those who participated in the conflict on the side of Ukrainian government. In April 2016, a draft law was registered in the *Verkhovna Rada*, proposing a radical option of nearly unconditional amnesty to people who were involved the ATO and committed crimes during that time.[51] Much more moderate provisions were included into the law on amnesty which was supposed to be linked with the celebrations of the 25th anniversary of Ukraine's independence.[52] The discussed problems of responsibility for crimes committed during the conflict were not central in this case. This document referred to a more general law setting up basic rules for applying amnesty in Ukraine,[53] and – as highlighted in the explanatory note accompanying the draft law – was regarded as an expression of the state's humanity in the execution of criminal penalties. According to the law, amnesty covered among others people who "defended the independence, sovereignty and territorial integrity of Ukraine, took part in anti-terrorist operation, and supported its implementation", but did

49 Draft law 'On avoiding prosecution and punishment of persons participating in the events in Donetsk and Luhansk oblasts', no. 5082, registered 16 September 2014.

50 Oksana Denisova, 'Chto na tom beregu?', *Zerkalo Nedeli*, 22 January 2016.

51 Draft law 'On amnesty for persons who at the time of committing crime took part in the anti-terrorist operation', no. 4519, registered 25 April 2016.

52 Draft law 'On amnesty in 2016', no. 4255, registered 17 March 2016.

53 Law of Ukraine 'On application of amnesty in Ukraine', no. 392/96, adopted 01 October 1996.

not commit any serious crime. The law thus referred also to participants of volunteer battalions who at the beginning of their functioning did not have an official status. The law was adopted on 7 July 2016, but then was vetoed by President Poroshenko. It may serve as additional evidence that the Ukrainian authorities will only take concrete steps in the field of amnesty when a more stable peace is achieved.

Special attention should be given to the issue of Ukraine's cooperation with the International Criminal Court (ICC). Not being a party of the Rome Statute, on 4 February 2015, the *Verkhovna Rada* of Ukraine adopted a declaration on the acceptance of jurisdiction of the ICC over alleged war crimes on the territory of Ukraine starting from 20 February 2014.[54] This refers to the annexation of Crimea and the occupation of parts of Donetsk and Luhansk *oblasts*. The declaration does not identify clearly the end date of the accepted jurisdiction. The appropriate declaration based on the parliamentary acceptance of the ICC jurisdiction over the events in Donbas was submitted by Ukraine's minister of foreign affairs Pavlo Klimkin to the Office of the Prosecutor on 8 September 2015.[55] It is noteworthy that despite the seven-months-long delay in fulfilment of necessary formalities enabling start of the preliminary examination of the case, Ukraine has sent several communications about allegations of crimes committed since March 2014. The ICC has openly stated that these events were beyond the Court's temporal jurisdiction.[56] During the period between the parliament's agreement to accept ICC jurisdiction over the Donbas case and its official lodging to the Court, Ukrainian authorities made several steps that could be seen as examples of institutional reform, having a potential impact on further cooperation with the ICC. In particular, in April 2015 a new law was adapted increasing responsibility for committing war crimes. According to it, the term of imprisonment was increased as punishment for abuse of power by military officials.[57] On 9 June 2015,

54 Statement of the Verkhovna Rada of Ukraine on recognition by Ukraine of jurisdiction of the International Criminal Court on crimes against humanity and war crimes committed by the high officials of the Russian Federation and leaders of terrorist organisations "DNR" and "LNR", which have led to serious consequences, and mass murder of Ukrainian citizens, no. 145-VIII, adopted 4 February 2015.

55 The full text of the document is available on the official website of the ICC: http://www.icc-cpi.int/iccdocs/other/Ukraine_Art_12-3_declaration_08092015.pdf.

56 International Criminal Court, The Office of the Prosecutor, 'Report on Preliminary Examination Activities 2014', 02 December 2014.

57 Law of Ukraine 'On amendments to the Criminal Code of Ukraine on the abuse of power by the military officials', no. 290-VIII, adopted 07 April 2015.

the Ukrainian government informed the Council of Europe about its derogation from the European Convention on Human Rights under Article 15 of the Convention.[58] It is an important legal step aimed at putting the responsibility for protection of human rights in the "ATO zone" on Russia, which is directly referred to as an invader occupying the integral territory of Ukraine.

While the decision of the ICC whether to start investigations of crimes committed during the Donbas conflict remains unknown, the general situation has revived the debate on the ratification of the Rome Statute.[59] It has revealed a paradox in the perception of the role of the ICC by the Ukrainian authorities. In their rhetoric, Ukrainian politicians usually speak enthusiastically about international criminal justice. This enthusiasm, however, is combined with the conviction that the eventual investigation will go in line with their perception and understanding of what is happening in Donbas. So, one cannot read anything about an objective investigation of the case in general in the transcript of the debate in the *Verkhovna Rada* that preceded the adoption of the mentioned declaration on 4 February 2015; instead there is an expectation that "Russian officials, and the heads of the LPR and DPR were prosecuted on the international level, in The Hague".[60] Also the declaration itself contains a suggestion on the responsibility of "the highest officials of the Russian Federation" (without mentioning particular names or positions) for committing crimes against humanity and war crimes on the territory of Ukraine – a step that obviously has no impact on the eventual investigation.

The draft amendment to the constitution on the judiciary system (discussed in more details in chapter 6) contains a provision allowing the ratification of the Rome Statute, although not earlier than three years after the amendment enters into force.[61] This is yet another paradox taking into account the discussed *ad hoc* adoption of the ICC jurisdiction. Despite enthusiasm towards international justice,

58 Art. 15 of the Convention reads as following: "In time of war or other public emergency threatening the life of the nation any High Contracting Party may take measures derogating from its obligations under this Convention to the extent strictly required by the exigencies of the situation, provided that such measures are not inconsistent with its other obligations under international law".

59 Leaving aside other reasons, Ukraine is obliged to ratify the Rome Statute in accordance with the Association Agreement with the European Union.

60 The transcript is retrieved from the official website of the Verkhovna Rada of Ukraine: http://rada.gov.ua/meeting/stenogr/show/5779.html (accessed 01 March 2016).

61 Draft law on amendments to the Constitution of Ukraine (on justice), no. 3524, registered 25 November 2015. All versions of the draft law are available in the online database of Ukrainian legislation: http://w1.c1.rada.gov.ua/pls/zweb2/webproc4_1?pf3511=57209.

the NSDC of Ukraine has expressed significant doubts about the advantage of the ratification of the Rome Statute. The main argument against ratification is the possibility for representatives of rebellious regions to accuse Ukraine for committing war crimes. Therefore, as the argument goes, ratification might have sense only in the case of similar steps taken by the Russian Federation. Similar arguments were publicly expressed by the leader of the BPP party and the Prosecutor General of Ukraine since May 2016 Yuriy Lutsenko. In an interview, Lutsenko stated that in the current situation, Ukraine has to fight rather than spend time in courts. In the same interview, he referred to the above-mentioned declarations on accepting the ICC's jurisdiction as cases of "partial ratification of the Rome Statute", thus showing insufficient knowledge in this field. Similar argumentation was presented by the representative of the President at a public hearing held by the Constitutional Court on the constitutional amendment to the judiciary system. According to him, the three year delay is a result of analysis and experience of other countries being in an armed conflict, in particular Georgia.[62]

These arguments may sound absurd and regarded as clumsy attempts to justify the lack of ratification for the public opinion. None of the most significant Ukrainian civil society activists and lawyers dealing with the issues of the rule of law and human rights have accepted such arguments as reasonable.[63] At the same time, some do not exclude that the Ukrainian authorities are afraid of prosecution for the ATO in the eastern *oblasts* of the country.[64] Such arguments by no means should be regarded as proof of crime, but rather as an anxiety of the long-lasting process as such and the reputational losses that may come with it. The situation can thus be similar to the one in 2000–2001 and President Kuchma's hesitations on the ratification of the Rome Statute.[65] Ukrainian experts also note

62 The recording of the hearing is available online: http://youtu.be/r_5-Jq4S6p0.

63 According to a brief survey of experts conducted by the NGO Human Rights Information Center. Opinions of experts are published on the website of the International Renaissance Foundation. Mykola Myrnyy, 'Ukrayina v pozytsiyi strausa shchodo ratyfikatsiyi Ryms'koho statutu', 04 February 2015, http://www.irf.ua/knowledgebase/news/ukraina_v_pozitsii_strausa_schodo_ratifikatsii_rimskogo_statutu/ (accessed 01 March 2016).

64 Author's interview with Stanislav Batryn, Kyiv-based human rights activist and expert of the NGO Public Commission for the Investigation and Prevention of Human Rights Violations in Ukraine (Kyiv, July 2015).

65 Among the reasons to withdraw from ratification of the Rome Statute was the fear of it by President Kuchma, who was allegedly involved in the selling of radars to Iraq despite international embargo.

that the Ukrainian authorities simply do not possess a full understanding of the logic of how the system of international justice works.[66]

The hesitation in the ratification of the Rome Statute combined with the *ad hoc* acceptance of the ICC jurisdiction, seemingly contradictory actions, illustrate how the Ukrainian authorities regard international criminal justice mechanisms primarily as a tool to internationalize the problem of the Donbas conflict, rather than as a tool that may help deal with the legacy of it. From the perspective of transitional justice, this means that there is no clear strategy to prosecute those responsible for committed war crimes. Otherwise, the engagement of the ICC, which is always complementary to the national judiciary system, should be treated as an element strengthening the policy of dealing with the crimes that took place during the conflict.

5.7. Effects and challenges

Two years after the beginning of the Donbas conflict, it is only possible to speak about the initial steps in formulating transitional justice policies that will eventually deal with the already visible legacy of the conflict. In accordance with theory, the Ukrainian authorities are focused on peacemaking and looking for compromise with the separatists (backed by Russia) that will create a framework for the design and implementation of transitional justice mechanisms in a narrow sense. At the same time, while the lack of peace is the most significant problem in the eyes of public opinion, there is no clear consensus around the final shape of the political solution to the conflict. As a result, no clear strategy on accountability for wrongdoings committed during the conflict exists. Therefore, there is a significant risk that this deficit may induce new political tensions when the priority of peacemaking is finally achieved. While the demand for transitional justice in the narrow sense is still weak, one can expect that the situation will change as soon as more or less stable "negative peace" is achieved, when disarmament and demobilization of combatants is fulfilled.

At that point, Ukrainian decision-makers will face several more specific dilemmas. First and foremost, one can expect a significant regional disproportion in the public expectations regarding how the *just* policies dealing with the legacy of the

66 Author's interview with prof. Volodymyr Vasylenko, International Law Chair at the National University of "Kyiv-Mohyla Academy". Prof. Vasylenko speaks about the "legal incompetence" in the field of international justice of Ukrainian authorities that came to power after the Euromaidan uprising as well as an unwillingness to provoke Russia (Kyiv, July 2015).

conflict should look like, reflecting current disproportions in how the conflict is perceived. The second challenge will be related to a balance between concessions given to wrongdoers in order to achieve peace (i.e. the final shape and conditions of amnesty) and compensation (as was mentioned above, compensation should not be understood only as a form of financial reparation in this case, but rather as any policy aimed at ensuring that the past suffering is not forgotten) to the victims. There are signals indicating that significant social tension in this field may appear. "After the terrorist attack in Paris, the US president said that the terrorists must be destroyed. Why their terrorists must be destroyed, and ours must be elected?"[67] This question, although illustrating a metaphoric exaggeration, is not without sense. It reflects the potential sentiments that will have political repercussions in the post-conflict Ukraine. In order to avoid them, the Ukrainian authorities have to clearly define a set of rules that would guide the policy of prosecution for war crimes after achieving peace. As Lars Waldorf states, in certain contexts even the wrongdoers may be interested in prosecutions, for they can serve the purpose of eliminating potential spoilers from the peace process.[68] A more pronounced cooperation with the ICC could help achieve this goal.

67 Oksana Syroid, 'Eshche raz ob osobennostyah "osobennostyey samoupravleniya"', *Zerkalo Nedeli*, 15 January 2016.
68 Waldorf, supra n 27 at 70.

6. Institutional reforms and constitutional amendments

6.1. Theoretical background

As mentioned at the beginning of the book, transitional justice policies, despite their predominantly retrospective nature, inevitably have a significant impact on the present and the future. Dealing with the "bad" legacy of the *ancien regime* is undoubtedly not an "art for the sake of art". It is especially evident in the case of political regimes declaring that their "normative anchor" is associated with democracy. Taking into account that violence and human rights abuses may have a structural nature, one should assume that transitional justice policies that act at the individual level (investigations and trials) may not be sufficient to eliminate the possibility that repressive institutions will automatically switch into the mode of functioning typical for democratic political systems. Some transitional justice policies, first and foremost vetting, have a strong impact not only on the affected individuals but also on the institutions as a whole. Therefore, they should be regarded as an element of institutional reform that goes beyond transitional justice in a narrow sense.[1] Indeed, as Alexander Mayer-Rieckh notes, "the multi-dimensional nature of the transitional reform challenge makes it generally necessary to complement vetting with other institutional reform measures and requires a holistic and coherent approach to institutional reform that may entail a complex, resource-intensive and lengthy process".[2]

In other words, the literature suggests that getting rid of "bad social capital" as a result of vetting policies should be followed by a change within the structure and basic rules governing the institutions in order to achieve sustainability of effects accomplished by the vetting. The scope of reform will undoubtedly depend on the normative criteria of the newly established political regime and contextual

---

1 Roger Duthie, 'Introduction', in *Justice as Prevention. Vetting Public Employees in Transitional Societies*, ed. Alexander Mayer-Riekh and Pablo de Greiff, (New York: Social Science Research Council, 2007), 31.

2 Alexander Mayer-Rieckh, 'On Preventing Abuse: Vetting and Other Transitional Reforms', in *Justice as Prevention. Vetting Public Employees in Transitional Societies*, ed. Alexander Mayer-Riekh and Pablo de Greiff, (New York: Social Science Research Council, 2007), 487.

conditions, such as opportunities, risks, needs, resource requirements and sustainability considerations.[3] On the other hand, institutional reform in itself may become a tool supporting the vetting process: the restructuring of an institution can be combined with the process of review of its employees; disbandment of the abusive institution and establishment in its place of a renewed one can be combined with the screening of candidates for an appointment.[4] Such supplement of more traditional vetting is especially important in circumstances of a significant level of institutional continuity – as in the discussed case of Ukraine.

Transitional reforms may refer not only to the changes of particular institutions, but to a much more fundamental change in the whole political system, as defined by the constitution. The significance of linkage between constitutional reform and transitional justice has been stressed by Ruti Teitel, who introduced the notion of "constitutional justice". Teitel's analysis of transitional justice is essentially normative (she refers to transition as a movement from less to more liberal political regime), hence the concept generally suggests that the constitutional process in a post-authoritarian society should be constructed in such a way that it establishes an overall framework to ensure accountability for past abuses. On a more general level, constitutionalism in transitional times plays the crucial role as a "rupture from the *ancien regime* and the founding of a new political order".[5] Constitutions, despite being aimed at securing the fundamental political arrangement in a given society and thus playing a rather counter-revolutionary role, can be designed with the aim to transform the reality in which the citizens live. This is the essence of the so-called transformative constitutionalism: setting up the basic legal framework for affirmation of new rules governing the functioning of society in accordance with the "normative anchor" of the incoming political regime.[6]

Understanding the process of constitutional change as closely related to the transitional justice policies is especially evident in the context of the necessity to deal with the legacy of the Donbas conflict. As mentioned above, Ukraine's post-Euromaidan transition can be regarded as a negotiated one. One of the points

---

3 Ibid., 504.

4 Ibid., 487–488.

5 Ruti G. Teitel, *Transitional Justice*, (New York: Oxford University Press, 2000), 194.

6 Probably the most widely discussed case of transformative constitutionalism in action is post-apartheid South Africa. See for example: Mashele Rapatsa, 'Transformative Constitutionalism in South Africa: 20 Years of Democracy', *Mediterranean Journal of Social Sciences*, vol. 5, no. 27 (2014).
The conditions, starting point and goals of South African transitional constitutionalism is, however, hardly comparable with the discussed case of Ukraine.

of the 21 February 2014 agreement between the former president Viktor Yanukovych and the opposition leaders contained the need to adopt a new constitution. At that moment, the need was associated with the public expectation to dismantle the specific political regime of so-called "oligarchic democracy" that can be regarded as a meta-reason for the outbreak of the Euromaidan and its consequences. In other words, the expectation to change the constitution was dictated by a conviction that there is a need to transform relations between the society and the political elites, not between different segments of society, and thus hardly corresponded with the concept of constitutional justice.

Along with the rise of separatism in the east of the country, the pressure to alter the basic "rules of the game" came also from the side of that part of the society who didn't support the Euromaidan ideas but who faced the consequences of the war in the east. This pressure helped formulate the idea of establishing a special status for Donbas and became associated with the wider process of constitutional change in particular with the process of decentralisation of power. As was discussed in chapter 5, the issue of special status for Donbas became an important element of the peace negotiations and thus should not be regarded exclusively as a subject of negotiations between different segments of Ukrainian society. What is important from the perspective of the topic of this book, the final shape of the constitutional agreement (which is far from known at the moment of writing the book) will most probably become an additional constraint for transitional justice policies aimed at dealing with the legacy of the Donbas conflict.

This chapter is devoted to the linkages between the transitional justice policies discussed in the previous chapters and the wider transitional reforms in Ukraine. First, a focus on the reforms of the law enforcement agencies and the judiciary system, which became supplements of the vetting policy, is provided. Next, the constitutional reforms on decentralisation, which is closely related with the Donbas conflict, will be in focus. In the former case, the reforms are a continuation of the initial transitional justice efforts while in the latter, the situation is the opposite – a reform driven by the goal of achieving peace may eventually define the scope and effectiveness of transitional justice policies. It is also important to note that this chapter is far from a comprehensive review of all the reforms being undertaken in Ukraine since the beginning of 2014; the focus here is primarily only on those elements which are related to the problems associated with transitional justice.

6.2. Reform of law enforcement agencies

The linkages between vetting and institutional reform have been introduced primarily in the law enforcement agencies, namely the prosecution and the police.

On 14 October 2014, the *Verkhovna Rada* adopted a new law on the prosecution.[7] The law is primarily aimed at bringing Ukraine's public prosecution system closer to the standards typical for EU member states, in particular eliminating the right of the prosecution to conduct so-called general supervision which in practice became one of the main channels of using the prosecution for repressive purposes. It also established a system of prosecutorial self-governance authorities. The law also removed from the prosecution the function of conducting prejudicial investigations, which was transferred to the newly established National Bureau of Investigation. What is important from the perspective of transitional justice, this law has disbanded all the existing district public prosecutor's offices and replaced them with local public prosecutor's offices. All the prosecutors from the disbanded offices willing to continue their service were obliged to go through the same assessment procedures as those without prosecutorial experience. In other words, the discussed law introduced a *de facto* screening of all the prosecutors at the lowest level (the one that has the most contact with ordinary citizens).

The most spectacular reform began almost year later on 2 July 2015 when the *Verkhovna Rada* adopted the law which initiated the gradual replacement of the old police, which was actually called militia (Ukr.: *міліція*) with the new law enforcement agency – the police (Ukr.: *поліція*).[8] As soon as law was published, the whole staff of the old militia was warned about the possibility of losing their position. Those who expressed a desire to continue their service in the new police should go through open competition. At the same time the law left the opportunity for former militia staff to be reappointed beyond the competition – a procedure clearly aimed at avoiding the problem of a governance gap which could be extremely dangerous in the specific circumstances of post-Euromaidan Ukraine. Furthermore, those previously fired from service on the basis of the law on lustration (discussed in chapter 3) had no possibility to work in the newly established police. Hence, the design of the transition from the old militia to the new police is the most spectacular example of an institutional reform supplementing previously introduced vetting policy – it basically implied the comprehensive replacement of the old institution.

There is also a link between institutional reforms and the specific feature of the post-Euromaidan vetting policy containing anti-corruption measures. As was stressed in chapter 3, vetting of public officers on the basis of their inability

7 Law of Ukraine 'On the Public Prosecutor's Office', no. 1697-VII, adopted 14 October 2014.

8 Law of Ukraine 'On National Police', no. 580-VIII, adopted 2 July 2015.

to explain the source of their assets may prove problematic due to the principle of presumption of innocence. The law establishing the main principles of the state anti-corruption policy of Ukraine for 2014–2017, adopted on 14 October 2014 (one month after the adoption of the lustration law) has openly admitted that Ukraine does not have an effective system of monitoring the authenticity of declarations regarding assets, incomes, expenditures and financial liabilities of public servants. Declarations are submitted in paper form to the agency which employs the officer. Audits are conducted by the tax authorities which do not have the proper level of independence to verify the declarations. A presentation of deliberately false information in the declaration does not entail criminal liability. As a result, the system actually encourages concealment of income and property by public servants.[9] It also means that provisions of the lustration law establishing the so-called "property lustration" remain ineffective. Without the system of verification of declarations, it is nothing more than a populist decoration added to the law in order to meet public expectations.

Several institutional changes have been introduced in order to solve this problem. First of all, on the same day of 14 October 2014, the National Anti-Corruption Agency (NACA) was established as a central executive body with the main task of preventing corruption among public servants. The agency has been given the right to verify the property declarations of all Ukrainian public officers, including monitoring of actual lifestyle of screened persons.[10] Also on the same day, the National Anti-Corruption Bureau of Ukraine (NABU) was set up. This is a new law enforcement body specialized in prevention, detection, investigation and disclosure of corruption crimes. Although it is not clearly articulated in the law, the main expectation of this institution is that it will deal with corruption amongst the highest officials.[11] Finally, the already mentioned law "On the Public Prosecutor's Office" has established a specialised anti-corruption prosecution within the structure of the Public Prosecutor's Office of Ukraine with the tasks of supervision of cases investigated by the NABU, maintenance of public prosecution and representation of interests of citizens and of the state in court in cases related to corruption.

Obviously, it is arguable whether the establishment of the mentioned institutions could actually be regarded as a reform linked to transitional justice policies.

9 Law of Ukraine 'On the principles of state anti-corruption policy of Ukraine (Anti-corruption strategy) in 2014–2017', no. 1699-VII, adopted 14 October 2014.

10 Law of Ukraine 'On prevention of corruption', no. 1700-VII, adopted 14 October 2014.

11 Law of Ukraine 'On National Anti-corruption Bureau of Ukraine', no. 1698-VII, adopted 14 October 2014.

Without a doubt, the logic of their tasks corresponds with the idea of "cleansing the government" from the persons involved in corruption and thus indirectly responsible for the poor situation of the country, fundamental for the post-Euromaidan vetting policy. On the other hand, whether these policies will correspond with transitional justice on a practical level will depend on how the newly established anti-corruption institutions function – namely, whether they will conduct a retrospective control and address abuses from the pre-Euromaidan period. Only in this case one may say that there is institutional reform that enforces the novel, anti-corruption element of vetting policy introduced in Ukraine.

6.3. Reform of the judiciary

It is difficult to exaggerate the significance of the judiciary in the whole process of implementation of transitional justice policies: transitional investigations should be finalized by court verdicts and the delivery of just decisions in doubtful vetting cases depend primarily on the courts. One might say that ultimately court decisions put a full stop in the implementation of transitional justice policies that define the impact of the latter on the political development of the state. The quality of the judiciary becomes crucial and the sequence of post-Euromaidan vetting (discussed in chapter 3) illustrates this. Nevertheless, one cannot speak about effective "cleansing" in Ukraine's judiciary system despite the fact that judges have become an object of two-level lustration.

Almost immediately after the adoption of the lustration law (which took place in September 2014), work on a fundamental reform of the judiciary system began. In October 2014, President Poroshenko created the Judiciary Reform Council (JRC), an advisory body with the task to develop the strategy of the mentioned reform. Thus, vetting was not considered as enough to achieve the goal of "rebooting" the judiciary system, an element of the state apparatus which enjoyed vast legal guarantees of independence. In essence, there was an understanding that a simple "cleansing" of institutions from the "bad" personnel may be not sufficient to overcome the primary problems of corruption and politicization typical for Ukraine's "oligarchic democracy". Furthermore, it became clear quite quickly that even the initial goal of "cleansing" the system from unreliable personnel may be difficult to achieve. As Oksana Syroid, at that time deputy head of parliament and member of the JRC, admitted, the lustration of judges did not work; furthermore, it might appear to be rather harmful due to the risk that the appeals of lustrated judges may be settled on at the level of the European Court of Human Rights. This, in turn, would not only lead to the restoration of vetted judges in their positions, but will also be associated with an obligation to pay reparations.[12] Putting aside the fact that such statements can be interpreted as a confession on the poor design of the vetting policies, it obviously signalled a change in the way of thinking about the basic goals of the vetting policy: these goals are expected to be achieved thanks to institutional reform.

The JRC proposed a two-stage approach to reform the judiciary. The first stage contains immediate changes in the legislation aimed at a renewal of trust in the judiciary. The second stage involves systemic changes in the legislation, including an amendment to the constitution, targeted at "comprehensive building of institutional capacity of relevant institutions".[13] Within the framework of implementation of the first stage of reform, the law "On the right to a fair trial" was adopted on 12 February 2015.[14] From the perspective of linkage with vetting policy, the law has introduced an obligatory "evaluation of qualification" (recertification) of all Ukrainian judges without exception. The whole process is to be organized by the High Qualification Commission for Judges, the institution whose personnel was previously "cleansed" on the basis of the law on lustration of judges. Judges, who have failed to go through the process of recertification, are removed from administration of justice and are obliged to participate in additional training at the National School of Judges of Ukraine.[15] Only after the second failed attempt to go through the recertification process, the High Qualification Commission recommends the High Council of Justice to fire the judge on the basis of breaking the oath. In other words, the law has introduced the third wave of screening of judges (after the law on lustration of judges and the main law on lustration). This time, however, it focused not on looking for particular "wrongdoings" allegedly conducted by the judges in the past, but on an assessment of their professional qualifications.

The second stage of reform started on 2 June 2016, when the *Verkhovna Rada* adopted an amendment to the constitution submitted by President Poroshenko in November 2015, which is aimed at conducting a fundamental reform of the judiciary system.[16] The amendment consolidates the scattered efforts undertaken

---

12 Interview with Oksana Syroid published on the official channel of Hromadske TV, 14 December 2015, http://youtu.be/hOI60xgrJpg (accessed 16 December 2015).

13 The strategy is available on the website of the Judicial Reform Council: http://jrc.org.ua/strategy (accessed 02 May 2016).

14 Law of Ukraine 'On the right to a fair trial', no. 192-VIII, adopted 12 February 2015.

15 The state institution with the special status aimed at providing high-quality staff for the judiciary system of Ukraine.

16 Law of Ukraine 'On amendments to the Constitution of Ukraine (on justice)', no. 1401-VIII, adopted 02 June 2016.

since the beginning of 2014 to reform the judiciary, but also touches upon public prosecution. Once again, the link was established between the reform and the logic of banning access to public service for undesirable persons. In particular, the amended constitution includes two new grounds to terminate the judge's tenure, which has emerged from the experience of the lustration of judges. The first is a violation of the obligation to prove the legality of possessed property – the provision aimed at making the "property lustration" of judges effective. The second is a lack of agreement to be moved to another court in the case of liquidation or reorganisation of a court where the judge works. This provision refers to the law discussed above "On the right to a fair trial", which gave the president the right to reorganise the courts. The amended constitution paves the way to use this mechanism as an additional tool to rid the system of undesirable judges. Obviously, such mechanism can be used also for purposes other than achieving the goals of transitional justice, which makes it potentially dangerous (for example, exerting pressure on judges). Additionally, the amended constitution establishes the groundwork for an assessment of the professional qualifications of the judges.

It is worth paying attention to the concurring opinions published by the Constitutional Court judges when the CCU accepted the discussed draft amendment.[17] The predominant doubt expressed by judges referred to potential threats to the principle of independence of judges that were imprinted in the draft amendment, in particular due to the process of assessment of professional qualifications. Also, some internal inconsistencies of the draft amendment have been noted along with the potential danger of unjustified influence of the president over the judiciary due to the right to liquidate and reorganise the courts. Another important doubt expressed by several judges does not refer to issues that have a direct connection with transitional justice, but results from the analysis of the draft amendment in a wider context of the political reality of the country. Namely, several judges have noted that the constitution of Ukraine prohibits amendments during war. While martial law has not been formally introduced, the actual situation, as well as a number of legal acts introduced by the Ukrainian authorities since March 2014 suggest that Ukraine is in a situation which is

---

17 The whole procedure requires acceptance of the proposed amendment by the Constitutional Court followed by two readings in the parliament. The amendment should be accepted by the ordinary majority of 226 in the first reading and by the constitutional majority of 300 MPs in the second reading. The readings cannot take place in one session of the *Verkhovna Rada*.

de facto similar to a state of war. Only one judge came to the conclusion that a lack of formal introduction of martial law is sufficient to eliminate doubts in this field.[18]

Finally, on the same day of 2 June 2016, the *Verkhovna Rada* adopted the law "On the judicial system and the status of judges",[19] which complements the adopted constitutional amendment. From the perspective of the linkages between the institutional reforms and vetting, the main edge of the law is on re-establishment of the Supreme Court (replacing the Supreme Court of Ukraine). Judges of the SCU have no guarantee of transfer to the newly established Supreme Court, although they are not banned from participating in competing for new positions. Importantly, the law has eliminated the obligation for the SC judges to possess experience working in the judiciary system, thus opening the way for jurists from outside the system. In this case, a logic different from the one applied in the course of the reform of public prosecution emerges: the fundamental renewal of the judiciary system is supposed to start at the highest level of institutional hierarchy. The law has established a clear system of qualification assessment which includes not only professional competences of judges, but also a systemic evaluation of the integrity and respect for ethic rules. In particular, along with property declarations, Ukrainian judges are now obliged to submit declarations of family connections once a year (aimed at revealing whether judges have close relations with other high state officials) and the so-called "declarations of honesty", in which judges are supposed to state that they are not engaged in any illegal activity (also submitted once a year). The law has additionally provided grounds for monitoring the judges' way of life in order to eliminate impunity for lodging false property declarations (which under the amended constitution can be grounds for losing tenure). Undoubtedly, these provisions are future-oriented, although at the initial phase of its implementation they may once again play the role of *de facto* vetting of judges who do not meet the newly defined criteria. In particular, the transitional provisions of the law introduced a clear obligation to go through the qualification assessment process for all judges appointed for a five year period[20] before the

18 Texts are retrieved from the website of the Constitutional Court of Ukraine: http://ccu.gov.ua/uk/doccatalog/list?currDir=299459 (accessed 20 February 2016).

19 Law of Ukraine 'On the judicial system and the status of judges', no. 1402-VIII, adopted 02 June 2016.

20 Prior to the amendment of the constitution discussed in this chapter, judges who were appointed for the first time, hold their office for the period of five years. After that, they received permanent positions. The amended constitution abolished this practice of the initial five-year "probation".

adoption of the law. With regard to other judges, such an assessment is not automatic but can be appointed by the High Qualification Commission.

Generally, this reform reflects the complexity of challenges related to vetting the judiciary system, which almost automatically becomes a systemic veto player[21] under the conditions of vetting aimed at reinforcing the principle of the rule of law. The assessment on the effectiveness of the whole reform is premature at the moment of writing the book. What can be done here is some preliminary conclusions about its effect reflected in the level of public trust in the judiciary system. According to a survey conducted by the Democratic Initiatives Foundation in December 2014, the overwhelming majority of Ukrainians support judicial reform. 46 percent of respondents regarded it to be one of the most urgent tasks to be fulfilled as soon as possible; 34 percent did not question the importance of the reform in general but were sure that more urgent problems needed to be solved; only 1.5 percent of Ukrainians did not see the need to reform the judiciary. At the same time, a majority of Ukrainians (46 percent) supported the idea of radical change that could lead to fundamental changes in the whole judiciary system of Ukraine, while 34 percent were sure that although the changes should be far-reaching, one should not change absolutely everything.[22] What should be underlined, however, is that there is much less confidence about whether there is a need to amend the constitution to achieve these goals. Ukrainians generally have a very limited understanding about the version of constitution which is at the moment in force. According to data published by Razumkov Centre (survey conducted in May 2015), less than nine percent of respondents gave an affirmative answer to the question on whether they are aware of the return to the 2004 version of the constitution that took place in February 2014; 40.5 percent admitted that they have heard something about it.[23] The obvious consequence is that there is no clear dominant preference in the public's mind as to whether the constitution should be changed at all: 40.6 percent of Ukrainians agreed that there was such a need, 23.3 percent stated that there was not and as much as 36 percent had no opinion regarding this issue.[24]

---

21 George Tsebelis, *Veto Players: How Political Institutions Work*, (Princeton: Princeton University Press, 2002).

22 Source: Democratic Initiatives Foundation, http://dif.org.ua/ua/publications/press-relizy/sudova-reforpertiv-.htm (accessed 21 May 2016).

23 Source: Razumkov Centre, http://www.razumkov.org.ua/ukr/poll.php?poll_id=1043 (accessed 21 May 2016).

24 Source: Razumkov Centre, http://www.razumkov.org.ua/ukr/poll.php?poll_id=1044 (accessed 21 May 2016).

6.4. Decentralisation

The annexation of Crimea and the escalation of the conflict in Donbas created a new context for the reform of the constitution, a need of which was obvious if Ukraine was to conclude a transition to a western-like democratic model. Along with strengthening the system of checks-and-balances, crucial for avoiding an unjustified concentration of power in the hands of the president, one of the essential problems to be solved through the means of constitutional reform was the decentralisation of power. It is important to note that issue of decentralisation did not first appear on the agenda in February 2014. It is an issue discussed by Ukrainian experts since the beginning of the 2000s, although mainly in the context of the ineffective governance that has hampered the socio-economic development of the country.[25] The rise of separatism has strongly politicised the issue. As mentioned in chapter 5, the corresponding constitutional reform became one of objects of the Minsk peace process and the notions of federalisation of Ukraine raised in the Russian media and by the separatists themselves could theoretically be regarded as compatible with the need for greater decentralisation. The problem with merging both concepts is derived from the radically different interests that stand behind both notions (see chapter 5).

The first step towards a new constitutional consensus that could serve as a foundation for the peacemaking and peacebuilding process, as well as advance the new political order, was taken on 16 September 2014 when the law "On special order of local self-government in certain areas of Donetsk and Luhansk oblasts"[26] (the term used to refer to the territories controlled by the self-proclaimed "people's republics") was adopted in order to commence the implementation of the initial Minsk agreements agreed upon several days earlier. Along with the already mentioned *de facto* amnesty (discussed in chapter 5), the law introduced a special regime for the period of three years. It foresaw the participation of the local self-government in appointing the heads of prosecutors' offices and courts, as well as the creation of a "people's militia" – a privilege no other Ukrainian region has. In addition, Ukraine has expressed commitment to design the so-called "agreement on economic, social and cultural development" as well as establish a special regime for business and investment, which would aim to facilitate the quick reconstruction of the destroyed economic and social

25 See: 'Prychyny, shcho obumovlyuyut' neobhidnist' provedennya administratyvnoyi reformy v Ukrayini', *Natsionalna bezpeka i oborona*, no. 5 (2000).

26 Law of Ukraine 'On special order of local self-government in certain areas of Donetsk and Luhansk oblasts', no. 1680-VII, adopted 16 September 2014.

infrastructure. The law was widely criticised, the most significant argument used by its opponents was that it essentially legalises the self-proclaimed authorities of the DPR and LPR and creates an obligation for the central government to finance the "republics". Ultimately, neither of the provisions came into force as they were conditioned by prior conduct of local elections in accordance with Ukrainian legislation. The general design of the document suggests that it was thought of as a provisional measure to allow the de-escalation of the conflict and focus on dialogue over a new constitutional consensus.

Despite the expectations of the Ukrainian authorities, the law did not contribute to the implementation of the first Minsk agreement. Both representatives of the "people's republics" as well as Russia continued insisting on more fundamental guarantees of the "special status" for the DPR and LPR within the Ukrainian state. In his interview to *Bild* magazine on 11 January 2016, Russian President Vladimir Putin openly stated: "First, the [Ukrainian] constitution has to be reformed. Only then can confidence building and border security follow".[27]

The process of constitutional reform was initiated on 3 March 2015, when President Poroshenko established the Constitutional Commission, with the task to prepare amendments to the constitution. On 1 July 2015, the president submitted to the parliament a proposed amendment which focused on the decentralisation of power. The vast majority of the proposed changes addresses the problem of excessive centralisation in Ukraine. The philosophy of changes presented in the explanatory note accompanying the initial version of the draft amendment[28] refers to the need of implementing the Association Agreement with the EU, which is regarded as an instrument for further transformation. The reformed system of self-government should thus meet the generally understood European standards in terms of self-government, in particular the principles of subsidiarity, universality and financial sustainability of local government. The explanatory note indeed mentions the Minsk protocol, but less directly: the president states only that the proposed draft amendment takes the latter into account. A detailed assessment of the proposed changes goes beyond the thematic scope of this book. It is important to note, however, that the basic idea of decentralisation proposed in the draft amendment focuses on strengthening the lowest level of

27 Nikolaus Blome, Kai Diekmann and Daniel Biskup, 'For me, it is not borders that matter', 11 January 2016, http://www.bild.de/politik/ausland/wladimir-putin/russian-president-vladimir-putin-the-interview-44092656.bild.html (accessed 12 January 2016).

28 Draft law on amendments to the Constitution of Ukraine (on decentralisation), no. 2217a, registered 01 July 2015. All versions of the draft law are available in the online database of Ukrainian legislation: http://w1.c1.rada.gov.ua/pls/zweb2/webproc4_1?pf3511=55812.

self-government – the local community (*hromada*). Communities should constitute the basic unit of the administrative-territorial structure of the country. Several communities form a province (*rayon*), provinces in turn are grouped into regions (replacing *oblasts*). This logic differs significantly from what is usually meant under the notion of federalisation, which assumes strengthening the level of regions in the first place while the issue of competences at lower levels of government virtually does not exist.

The dispute surrounding the proposed changes to the constitution have risen, however, not from the nuances of administrative-territorial structure of Ukraine, but from one sentence that is to guarantee the aforementioned special status of the "certain parts of Donetsk and Luhansk *oblasts*". This sentence is also crucial from the perspective of linkages between the reform and transitional justice policies referring to the Donbas conflict. It reads as follows: "Specific arrangements for self-government in some parts of Donetsk and Luhansk oblasts shall be set forth in a separate law".[29] It was the final point of transitional provisions of the bill on introducing changes to the constitution. The obvious logic behind it was to provide a constitutional ground for the mentioned law from 16 September 2014, but also to include the "certain parts" into a regular system of self-government upon expiry of the law.

On 15 July 2015, President Petro Poroshenko submitted a revised version of the same reform. Among the significant changes was the transfer of the mentioned rule on "certain areas of Donetsk and Luhansk *oblasts*" from transitional provisions of the bill to transitional provisions of the constitution itself. As a result, should the proposed amendments be adopted, the "special order of self-government" would gain constitutional status, although the essence of the specificity would remain undefined in the constitution. This version of the bill became the basis for further procedures of the amendment. On 16 July 2015, the parliament submitted the draft amendments to the Constitutional Court, which has affirmed it on 31 July 2015. On 31 August 2015 the *Verkhovna Rada* adopted the draft amendments in the first reading. The second reading has not yet taken place at the time of writing the book.

This legal manoeuvring is undoubtedly linked with efforts to find a formula of distribution of power within the political system of Ukraine that would be accepted by all sides of the conflict, and thus play a foundational role for the new

---

29 In original: "Особливості здійснення місцевого самоврядування в окремих районах Донецької і Луганської областей визначаються окремим законом". The translation is taken from the official documents of the Council of Europe.

political order. The discussed constitutional amendment can be a good example of an attempt to implement what Ruti Teitel calls transitional constitutionalism which "not only is constituted by the prevailing political order but also is constitutive of political change".[30] That desired effect (from the perspective of the Ukrainian authorities), however, may be difficult to achieve.

Although the verdict of the Constitutional Court was affirmative, its assessment referred only to the question as to whether the proposed draft amendment limits the guaranteed rights and freedoms of citizens. The judges have issued four concurring opinions, only one of which does not refer to the provision of "specific arrangements for self-government". Similar to the discussed case of the reform of the judiciary system, the judges noted that there is grounds to speak about Ukraine being *de facto* in a state of war. Judge Mykola Melnyk has stressed, that although the provision does not limit explicitly the existing rights and freedoms, the lack of precision about how the "specific arrangements" should look combined with the possibility to specify them with an ordinary law, creates a risk that these arrangements may limit the rights and freedoms in the future, thus creating unacceptable inequality among citizens of Ukraine. It might also lead to *de facto* withdrawal of the territories from the jurisdiction of Ukraine. Also according to Judge Segiy Sas, the provision may lead to a situation where the system of local self-government in Ukraine is diversified. Most judges agree that despite being part of transitional provisions, the discussed rule will take on a permanent nature.[31] The permanent nature of the discussed draft provision referring to separatist-controlled territories was confirmed in the opinion of the Venice Commission.[32]

The Ukrainian public opinion is far from being unequivocal in their assessment of the proposed constitutional amendment. In August 2015, the idea of providing the self-proclaimed "people's republics" with the special status guaranteed by the constitution was accepted by 36.5 percent of Ukrainians, while almost 40 percent rejected it and as much as 24 percent did not have an opinion.[33] A similar dispersion of opinions was observed with respect to the proposed provision in the draft

---

30 Teitel, supra n 5 at 191.

31 Texts are retrieved from the website of the Constitutional Court of Ukraine: http://ccu.gov.ua/uk/doccatalog/list?currDir=281857 (accessed 20 January 2016).

32 European Commission for Democracy through Law, 'Opinion on the Temporal Validity of Draft Transitional Provision 18 of the Constitution of Ukraine', no. CDL-AD(2015)030, 23–24 October 2015.

33 Source: Razumkov Centre, http://www.razumkov.org.ua/ukr/poll.php?poll_id=1054 (accessed 21 May 2016).

constitutional amendment regulating the status of the DPR and LPR ("Specific arrangements for self-government in some parts of Donetsk and Luhansk oblasts shall be set forth in a separate law"). It was supported by 24.4 percent of Ukrainians; 44.4 percent expressed a negative opinion and 31.4 percent had no opinion at all.[34]

6.5. Effects and challenges

"Lustration must never replace structural reforms aimed at strengthening the rule of law and combatting corruption",[35] the Venice Commission stated in its opinion on Ukraine's law on lustration. To a large extent, the reforms described in this chapter can be regarded as an implementation of this recommendation (with the exception of the decentralisation process, which obviously has no link with the implementation of administrative justice and thus should be considered separately). However, there are no comprehensive statistical data allowing for a comparison of the scale of the purge of public institutions with the scale of the purge achieved as a result of vetting policies. Yet, there are some indicators that may be helpful in assessing the quantitative effects of these reforms.

When speaking about the reform of the prosecution, the procedure of reassessment of employees of local prosecution offices was meant to let "fresh blood" into the system of public prosecution and thus leaving behind the unwanted representatives of the past. In reality, the General Prosecutor Office has limited the possibility of independent jurists (the ones who were not employees of the prosecution) to participate in the competition for jobs in the renewed local offices. As a result, the scale of "cleansing" was rather moderate: in the case of heads of local prosecutors' offices, 80 percent kept their positions. At both the regional and central level, the staff within the prosecutors' offices remained unchanged.[36] For that reason, the idea of a bottom-up approach to reform within the prosecution was widely criticized by the proponents of the reform. In particular, one of the strongest arguments states that the establishment of strong self-governance in the circumstances when the prosecution is dominated by the "old cadre" may

34 Source: Razumkov Centre, http://www.razumkov.org.ua/ukr/poll.php?poll_id=1060 (accessed 21 May 2016).

35 European Commission for Democracy through Law, 'Final opinion on the law on government cleansing (Lustration law) of Ukraine', no. CDL-AD(2015)012, 19 June 2015.

36 Interview with Maryna Tsapok, expert of the NGO Reanimation Package of Reforms, for Hromadske TV: https://youtu.be/laEb5mqhoOA.

eventually lead to a conservation of the system and increase the immunity of the institution from further reforms.[37] The first conference of the prosecutors aimed at the emergence of self-governance took place at the beginning of May 2016, hence the actual impact of it on the reform of the prosecution will be possible only after further research.

In the case of the police reform, the interior minister Arsen Avakov has assessed that around seven percent of the "former ones" were not allowed to go through open competition. The competition as such resulted in the rejection of around 25 percent of the command staff and 12 percent of the general staff from the old militia.[38] At first glance, the effects appear more impressive than in the case of the prosecution reform. However, in this case the ministry of interior faced the problem of mass cancellation by courts of the competition results which are unfavourable for the former militia officers willing to continue service in the renewed police. Paradoxically, however, this phenomenon may be regarded as an indicator of courts acting in line with the provisions of the law on the police. As noted by Oleksandr Banchuk, a jurist working at the NGO Centre of Policy and Legal Reform, the root of the of the problem lies in the fact that most police officers were reappointed beyond the competition, on the basis of a procedure designed to avoid the problem of governance gap. This took place before the ministry of interior adopted the executive document regulating the procedure of certification of police officers. As a result, the certification formally took place on the basis of a provision of the law that establishes the procedure of assessment of officers applicable in the cases of appointment to higher positions, degradation or removal from service (thus designed for "ordinary" functioning of the police, not a transitional period between the old militia and the new police).[39]

---

37 Such idea was expressed, among others, by Vitaliy Kasko, deputy Prosecutor General of Ukraine in May 2014–February 2016. Mr. Kasko was one of the main proponents of the reform of the prosecution but resigned from the office because of the alleged inability to fight corruption within the institution. The GPOU has in turn started a criminal investigation against him. Kasko is suspected of illegally receiving two apartments. After leaving the GPOU, Mr. Kasko has joined Transparency International in Ukraine. See interview with Vitaliy Kasko for Hromadske. TV: https://youtu.be/WAI6X8kxUuk.

38 Sergey Rahmanin, 'Glava MVD Arsen Avakov: "My zdes vse ne svyatye"', *Zerkalo Nedeli*, 12 February 2016.

39 Oleksandr Banchuk, 'Chomu suddi masovo ponovlyuyut zvilnenyh politseyskyh, i yak tse zupynyty', *Ukrayinska Pravda*, 05 May 2016.

The described problem that occurred in the process of the police reform illustrates once again the significance of the courts in the whole process. It is also a good example of the need for accuracy when reforms are being formulated as a way to achieve goals typical for the administrative justice through means less controversial from the perspective of the rule of law. This remark refers also to the earlier-discussed judicial reform, which was still in the process of formulation at the moment of writing the book. Several attempts to approach the problem of "cleansing" in the judicial system only demonstrate that it is extremely challenging to renew the judiciary system without exerting political influence over it. As stressed by CCU Judge Stanislav Shevchuk:

> "Undoubtedly, after so many years of attempts to put the judicial system under control of certain political forces, there is an urgent problem of restoration of trust in the judiciary, the cleansing of it from political nominees and factors of corruption. Nevertheless, this process cannot be a task in itself, furthermore, it cannot be conducted under the influence of the logic of 'revolutionary expediency'. It is enough to study Ukrainian history of the 20th century to understand what it may lead to".[40]

Another important problem demonstrated by the attempt to reform Ukraine's judiciary system was stressed by CCU Judge Sergiy Sas:

> "Reform of one branch of power apart from the others is impossible. Generally, one should speak about the need to create the branches of power and normative regulation of mechanisms of interactions between them: cooperation, mutual control and containment from excessive empowerment. Without any doubt, first of all it is important to determine the type of political system in order to build the structure of state power on that basis".[41]

Indeed, these words can also be a good commentary on the attempts to embed the special status of the self-proclaimed "people's republics" into an amendment to the constitution on decentralisation. Although this step may be regarded as a concession necessary to cease the violence, in the long run the actual results may appear counter-productive in establishing a long-lasting and just peace. In particular, should the proposed amendment come into force, there will be no guarantee that the post-conflict transitional justice policies will be fully implemented on the whole territory of Ukraine. Unsurprisingly, the draft amendment on decentralisation has provoked social protests. On 31 August 2015, the day when

40 Text retrieved from the website of the Constitutional Court of Ukraine: http://ccu.gov.ua/uk/doccatalog/list?currDir=299459 (accessed 20 February 2016).

41 Text retrieved from the website of the Constitutional Court of Ukraine: http://ccu.gov.ua/uk/doccatalog/list?currDir=299459 (accessed 20 February 2016).

the amendment was adopted by the *Verkhovna Rada* in the first reading, protests took place in front of the parliament building, resulting in several deaths. The lack of a clear acceptance of the amendment by the public confirms that there is a potential for even further protests by the ones who regard the provision as an unjustified concession to the "people's republic" and Russia. This stands in clear contrast with the clear acceptance of the proposals to reform the judiciary. The potential effect of the latter is much clearer and the justice achieved through its means is thus more tangible.

In any case, from the perspective of reinforcing democracy, any attempt to supplement transitional justice policies with corresponding reforms would make no sense if it does not lead to an increase of public trust in the affected institutions.

7. Conclusions: Lessons learned from Ukraine's transitional justice policies

7.1. Ukraine's political development after the Euromaidan

The period of time covered in this book – the slightly more than two years that have passed since the end of the Euromaidan protests – was an extremely dynamic period in political terms. Although it was declared that "Ukraine returned to a democratic trajectory in 2014",[1] the movement along this trajectory appeared to be uneven, and the final destination remains uncertain. An objective assessment of policies analysed in the chapters above requires putting them into a wider context.

The start of 2016 in Ukraine was marked by an intense political crisis illustrated by tensions within the governing coalition. After a failed attempt to dismiss the government in February 2016, the political parties of *Batkivshchyna* and *Samopomich* left the governing coalition (another minor partner, the Radical Party, did so already in December 2015). As a result, the government remained without support of an absolute majority of MPs – the remaining fractions of Petro Poroshenko's Block (BPP) and the People's Front lacked the necessary 226 mandates. Due to declining public support for both these biggest fractions, neither was interested in early elections. As a result of a frantic search for a way out of the crisis, Arseniy Yatsenyuk resigned as prime minister in April 2016 and a new government was established, headed by Volodymyr Hroysman, the former speaker of the parliament and a close ally of President Poroshenko. Formally, the governing coalition remained unchanged. The deficit of votes, which was deepened by the refusal of some members of the BPP to support the new government, was compensated by the backing of two minor fractions, neither of which has formally joined the governing coalition: Will of People (Ukr.: *Воля Народу*) and Revival (Ukr.: *Відродження*). Both groups consist of MPs close to the already non-existent Party of Regions and are regarded as representations of oligarchic interests. This political manoeuvre has become an important indicator of the ever present strength of oligarchs and their impact on key political decisions in the country.[2] One should add here that the whole crisis was accompanied by

1 Freedom House, 'Nations in Transit 2015. Ukraine', https://freedomhouse.org/report/nations-transit/2015/ukraine (accessed 16 May 2016).

2 For example: Maxim Eristavi, 'Now We Know Who Really Runs Ukraine', *Foreign Policy*, 17 February 2016.

the withdrawal of ministers who were considered to be leading reformists and guarantors of a transparent allocation of foreign aid in the Yatsenyuk "kamikaze cabinet". To a large extent, the crisis itself was triggered by the resignation of Economy Minister Aivaras Abromavičius, who publicly accused representatives of the government of yielding to pressure from oligarchic "clans" (in other words, political corruption). Publicly debated ideas of establishing a technocratic government[3] headed by Natalie Jaresko, the Finance Minister in Yatsenyuk's cabinet, quickly lost support in the parliament.

The unacceptability of such solutions is generally explained by the aspiration of the "clans" to maintain control over "financial flows" (i.e. government spending) in exchange for support provided in parliament. In other words, we observe a continuation of the tradition of rent-seeking based on close connections between business and politics. Although the direct connection between a particular government's decision and the benefits of a particular oligarchic "clan" should rather be a task for investigative journalism, the general expectations here is as follows: "It is the oligarchs who will be the main beneficiaries of a weak prime minister who is forced to rely on a weak coalition. Every vote will involve a payment, whether it comes in the form of a job, access to funds, a contract, or a state-owned enterprise."[4] All in all, these developments create a firm basis to state that during the discussed period of time, the problem of the state's lack of impartiality vis-à-vis strong oligarchic clans was far from solved.

In examining the quality of the rule of law, an unequivocal assessment may be difficult to make. Although the idea of the rule of law as such is clear, it is a challenging concept to measure. The approach taken in this book is inspired by the tradition of democratic audits in which three factors are taken into account: quality of legislation, institutional infrastructure (understood as organization and effectiveness of courts and the public prosecutor's office) and prestige of law (understood as compliance with the applicable legal provisions and the level of tolerance for actions resulting in breaking the law).[5] On the one hand, the analysis of

3 The term "technocratic government" became extremely popular in the Ukrainian public discourse, referring to government that consists of professionals rather than politicians. In specific Ukrainian conditions, it reflects primarily the will to eliminate politics popularly understood as a game between influential oligarchs.

4 Sergii Leshchenko, 'Why I'm Pessimistic about Ukraine's New Government', weblog on Atlantic Council, 20 April 2016, http://www.atlanticcouncil.org/blogs/new-atlanticist/why-i-m-pessimistic-about-ukraine-s-new-government (accessed 16 May 2016).

5 Radosaw Markowski et al., *Democratic Audit of Poland 2014*, (Frankfurt am Main: Peter Lang Edition, 2015), 33.

particular transitional justice policies in itself presented in the previous chapters of the book provides us with a number of examples that can serve as indicators of the shortcomings in the fields of all three rule of law factors. The contradictions in the lustration law, controversies expressed by some of the CCU judges regarding draft amendments to the constitution or loopholes in new laws on the public prosecution and the national police, hampering the renewal of personnel of these institutions are prominent examples of poor quality of legislation. These cases also provide numerous instances of controversial court decisions that have an impact on the whole process of implementation of transitional justice policies, which are indicators of an improper functioning of the judiciary. Furthermore, only two percent of Ukrainians actually inform the law enforcement agencies about the instances of corruption[6] – a clear indicator of the high level of tolerance for breaking the law, especially taking into account that corruption is regarded as the most significant problem in Ukraine and an obstacle for its development. On a more aggregate level, the World Justice Project in its 2015 edition of the Rule of Law Index has scored Ukraine with 0.48 points on a scale from 0 (low quality of rule of law) to 1 (high quality of rule of law), placing the country at the seventieth position out of 102 states assessed.[7] This indicator, however, does not fully show the dynamics due to the fact that the publication is the first iteration (with no previous editions).

Corruption and criminal justice are indicated as the most problematic spheres. In these particular problematic fields, the lack of progress was noted also by Freedom House.[8] At the same time, Transparency International, despite the already mentioned pessimistic data reflecting the level of tolerance for corruption, has noted the tendency of growth in the amount of Ukrainians declaring their readiness to inform law enforcement agencies about cases of corruption. It would thus be just to sum up, that despite a lack of significant progress by Ukraine in the field of quality of the rule of law two years after Ukraine's last transition, there are phenomena allowing for a belief that the situation may improve in the near future.

In terms of democratic accountability, in 2014, Ukraine conducted early presidential and parliamentary elections which were recognized as free and fair, despite the fact that the loss of control over a significant part of territory due to annexation

6 Transparency International Ukraine, 'V Ukrayini pochav formuvatysya progresyvnyy prosharok suspilstva – vykryvachi', http://ti-ukraine.org/news/oficial/6030.html (accessed 16 May 2016).

7 Source: World Justice Project, http://worldjusticeproject.org/rule-of-law-index (accessed 16 May 2016).

8 Freedom House, supra n 1.

of Crimea and the rise of the "people's republics" in the east of the country led a significant part of population to be deprived of the right to vote. The local elections held in October 2015 were also recognized as free and fair. In this case, however, there were much more audible accusations of falsifications applied primarily by the new authorities.[9] Nevertheless, Freedom House has improved Ukraine's score in the field of democratic governance "due to the stabilization of the national political situation and the survival of basic democratic institutions following the constitutional and security crises" and "due to the first visible progress in setting up new local communities under recently adopted legislation".[10] Another phenomenon, significant from the point of view of democratic accountability, is a further strengthening of the civil society which is visible in the active attempts of NGOs to participate in the policymaking process (also in the field of transitional justice, as was presented in the previous chapters) and the unprecedented rise of volunteer movements along with the escalation of the Donbas conflict. As was noted by Tadeusz Olszański, "from the political point of view, it is important that the volunteers' activities, both armed (soldiers) and civilian, have shown that the people can force the state and the authorities to do something without overthrowing it".[11]

Finally, it should be clearly stressed that Ukraine's movement along Fukuyama's three axes of political development (evolution of impartial state, rule of law and democratic accountability)[12] happens in the circumstances of an armed conflict, which additionally boosts the power of local oligarchs because of the need for a weak central government for support in the regions, especially those bordering Crimea and Donbas.[13] Another important circumstance is the severe economic crisis. Ukraine's GDP fell by seven percent in 2014 and by twelve percent in 2015; during the same time, the Ukrainian currency lost about seventy percent of its value against U.S. dollar.[14] These indicators explain the attention paid by Ukrainians to economic problems at the cost of other important issues.

---

9 Tadeusz A. Olszański, 'The local government elections in Ukraine', *Centre for Eastern Studies Analyses*, 04 November 2015.

10 Ibid.

11 Tadeusz A. Olszański, 'Aftermath of the Maidan. Ukrainian society two years after the revolution', *Centre for Eastern Studies Commentary*, 04 March 2016.

12 See footnote 8 in chapter 1.

13 Andrew Wilson, 'Survival of the Richest: How Oligarchs Block Reform in Ukraine', *European Council on Foreign Relations Policy Brief*, April 2016, 6.

14 'The Ukrainian economy is not terrible everywhere', *The Economist*, 20 January 2016.

Figure 10: General assessment of the situation in the country by Ukrainians

Source: Razumkov Centre, *Otsinka hromadyanamy sytuatsiyi v krayini. Rezultaty sotsiolohichnoho doslidzhennya*, (Kyiv 2016).

This complicated situation has significantly impacted public attitudes of Ukrainians. The overall assessment of the situation in the country has returned to the pre-Euromaidan level (Figure 10). Trust in public institutions remains extremely low, with the new National Police, army and the National Guard as exceptions. Most public trust was given to the mentioned volunteer organisations[15] (Figure 11). Last but not least, the electoral support of the two parties which make up the governing coalition has declined in the spring of 2016 to 11.9 percent in the case of BPP and as little as 0.8 percent in the case of the People's Front. The Opposition Block, the direct successor of the Yanukovych's Party of Regions became the leader of electoral preferences, although the scale of support for this new leader

15 Volunteer organisations, undoubtedly, belong to the category of NGOs. The motivation to separate them in a cited survey is dictated by clear separation of these types of organisations in Ukrainian public discourse. The term "NGOs" usually refer to organisations involved in policy analysis and advocacy, predominantly working with state institutions at the central level. The term "volunteer organisations" usually refers to organisations, whose work is predominantly in the field and is related to the outcomes of the Donbas conflict (support for IDPs, providing necessary equipment for the army etc.).

(12.3 percent) reflects general disappointment with the political elites rather than a rise of revanchist moods.[16]

Figure 11: Balance of trust in public institutions (April 2016)[17]

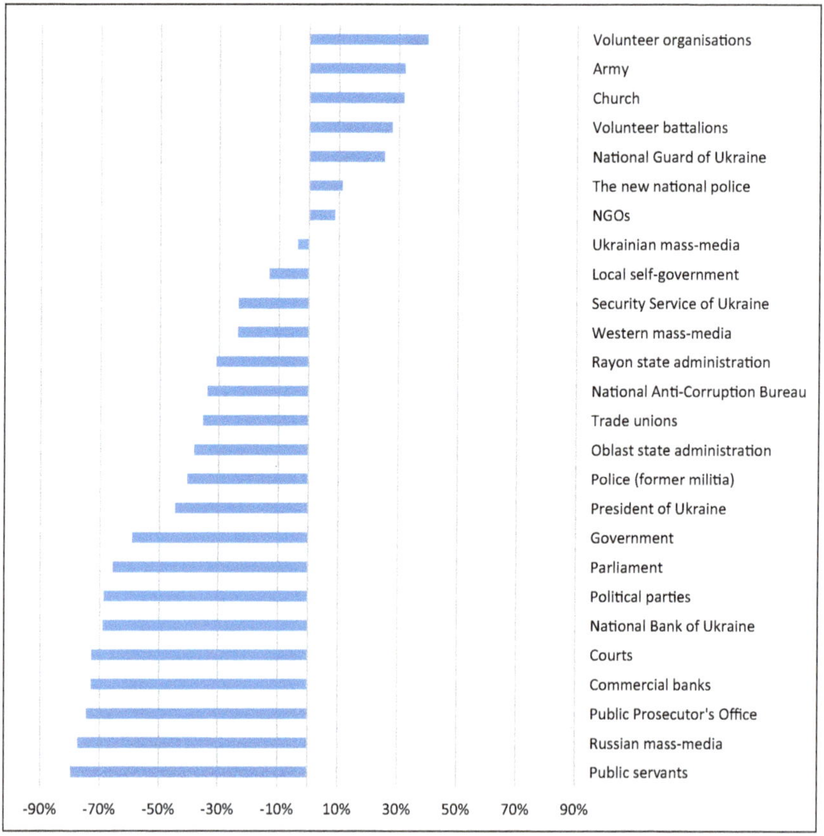

Source: Razumkov Centre, *Otsinka hromadyanamy sytuatsiyi v krayini, stavlennya do suspilnyh instytutiv, elektoralni orientatsiyi. Rezultaty sotsiolohichnoho doslidzhennya*, (Kyiv, 2016).

16 Source: Razumkov Centre, *Otsinka hromadyanamy sytuatsiyi v krayini, stavlennya do suspilnyh instytutiv, elektoralni orientatsiyi. Rezultaty sotsiolohichnoho doslidzhennya*, (Kyiv, 2016).

17 The difference between the share of those who trust to those who do not trust each particular institution.

7.2. Explaining the patchwork of transitional justice policies

The presented picture of the trajectory of Ukraine's post-Euromaidan political development suggests that the country's expected transition towards democracy is hampered primarily by what can be called the "burden of the past"; first and foremost the continuous influence of the oligarchic "clans" on state policies. Having this in mind, it is possible to assess the extent transitional justice policies (the general task of which is exactly dealing with the "burden of the past") helped overcome this problem.

The first general conclusion that emerges from the analysed transitional justice policies is that they are closely intertwined with each other. The same problems are often addressed by different policies. Taking this interrelationship into account, one can better explain the complicated puzzle of Ukraine's transitional justice as well as draw more specific conclusions about the effect of these policies' implementation. All of the discussed policies share the basic features of transitional justice measures: their implementation is motivated by a combination of political and legal considerations; and they address the problems of large-scale violence and human rights abuse (both direct and structural). What differentiates them, however, is the period of Ukraine's transition being the main object of certain policies and the specific problems that generated the mentioned human rights abuse during that particular stage of transition. On this basis, one can distinguish three clusters of policies, which can be called the dimensions of transitional justice in Ukraine.

The **first dimension** of Ukraine's transitional justice is defined by what was called in the introduction as the country's first and most obvious transition that took place in 1991. This dimension is also the most similar to transitional justice policies in other CEE states, as it is targeted at the legacy of the already distant past of communist rule. The foundation of this dimension is made up of the policy of historical justice, supplemented by elements of lustration (the main goal of which is far from "cleansing" state institutions from former Soviet *apparatchiks* and secret service collaborators). Taking into account that the policy is being implemented 25 years after the fall of communism, this dimension of transitional justice, in practical terms, can be expected to exclude certain values and attitudes from the public space that are associated primarily with the Soviet past but that were also utilized by some political forces after 1991. At the same time, one can hardly expect that vetting of former Soviet officers may have a significant impact on the political developments of the country simply because the scale of their presence in public institutions a quarter of a century after the transition is not significant. Indeed, the existing research on post-communist transitional justice suggest that the window of opportunity for such hard measures (in the sense of policies that affect certain persons or categories of citizens, in particular lustration) that may have a positive impact on supporting trust in government and democratisation closed around 15 years after the regime change.[18] In other words, putting a main focus within this dimension on symbolic measures can be regarded as a wise step. Within the period of time covered in this book, there was no significant attempts to sabotage or undermine the implementation of policies focused on a symbolic break with the communist past (in particular, the process of de-communisation). This is not to say that the policies have not caused controversies, they certainly have. Furthermore, one cannot exclude that further implementation of the policy will trigger more conflict in a society divided by attitudes to the values addressed within this dimension of transitional justice. A focus on symbolic issues also means that the impact of the discussed measures on political development can hardly be observable in such a short period of time: at the macro-level of the whole society, a reassessment of the already distant past will take place not at the moment when some symbols of that past are removed from the public space, but because the incoming generations will be raised in new narratives.

The **second dimension** of Ukrainian transitional justice policies is defined by the Euromaidan protests as a threshold separating, the "fallen tyranny" of the Yanukovych presidency from the mentioned "return to the democratic trajectory". In other words, these are policies that are designed by the post-Euromaidan authorities to address the abuses of human rights committed by their direct predecessors: mass violence that took place during the Euromaidan protests but also the less obvious structural violence (predominantly economic) being the informal feature of the specific political system that emerged after 1991 and culminated under the presidency of Viktor Yanukovych. The foundation of this dimension is constituted by investigations and trials of Euromaidan-related violence, the vetting of state officials who worked under Yanukovych and the ones involved in corruption. It is also supplemented by institutional reforms of the judiciary and law enforcement agencies.

This dimension of transitional justice differs significantly from other well-studied post-communist cases. Unlike the 1991 transition from Soviet rule to a pluralist but unconsolidated democracy, which can be described as a transplacement in Huntington's sense, the 2014 transition was accompanied by violence

18 Cynthia M. Horne, 'The Timing of Transitional Justice Measures', in *Post-Communist Transitional Justice. Lessons from Twenty-Five Years of Experience*, ed. Lavinia Stan and Nadya Nedelsky (New York: Cambridge University Press, 2015), 142.

and had more elements of regime breakdown,[19] after which the supporters of the old regime were quickly replaced by the former opposition. However, this happened without a fundamental change in the formal rules regulating the functioning of the political system. The incoming regime has not established a new constitution following the logic of "revolutionary necessity"; instead, it restored an older version of it, the one under which the former president, later accused of usurpation of power, was democratically adopted. The legitimacy of laws adopted by the *ancien regime*, (even the most brutal ones, like the so-called "dictatorial laws") was not questioned, the parliament conducted only a normal legislative procedure to abolish them. In such circumstances, this dimension of transitional justice can basically be regarded as an attempt to weaken the "path dependency"[20] of Ukraine's post-1991 development; to break with the informal rules that constituted circumstances conductive for the development of the "oligarchic democracy" and ultimately allowed Yanukovych and his entourage to transform the state into a private mechanism of enrichment. From the perspective of transitional justice policies, the issue of retrospectivity is missing. In other words, it is not the new regime who defines the illegality of wrongdoings addressed within the discussed dimension of transitional justice. Starting from abuse of power and economic crimes and ending with ordinary corruption – neither of these acts could be regarded as legal before February 2014. In other words, within this dimension we deal rather with retrospective crime control, a situation when law is executed with a delay (with the exception of mass killings in the centre of Kyiv in February 2014, the investigation of which started without delay, and the element of lustration policy banning public employees serving under Yanukovych, which is not a crime). The political component of transitional justice in this case paradoxically refers to a decision that the existing law should be applied while new legal provisions are aimed primarily not at establishing responsibility for past deeds, but to introduce mechanisms enabling more effective control over acts that were illegal when committed.

One can assume that it is exactly in this dimension that the most direct impact on political development can take place: investigations finalized by court verdicts should demonstrate that a high position in the state is by no means a guarantee of impunity; vetting should purge state institutions from the "bad social capital" that may be the main source of resistance against the introduction of

19 Samuel Huntington, *The third wave. Democratization and the late twentieth century*, (Norman: University of Oklahoma Press, 1991), 23–57.

20 Paul Pierson, 'Increasing Returns, Path Dependence, and the Study of Politics', *The American Political Science Review*, vol. 94, no. 2 (2000): 251–267.

rules brought on by the incoming political regime; institutional reforms should supplement these efforts and consolidate changes achieved by the removal of unwanted staff by altering the procedures. Despite a seemingly comfortable situation for the gradual decrease on the level of patrimonialization of the state and the enforcement of the rule of law, what can be observed in practice is a very moderate (in quantitative terms) result in both the post-Euromaidan investigations and trials as well as the vetting process. The discussed institutional reforms, designed in a way to reinforce the effects of the vetting policy, have not changed the situation significantly. At the same time, as was presented in Figure 11, the level of trust in most public institutions remains extremely low.

Finally, the **third dimension** of Ukraine's transitional justice is the most specific one. It is defined by the already obvious legacy of the ongoing Donbas conflict and focuses primarily on the prosecution of crimes committed during the conflict, deliberations about possible amnesties supplemented by elements of lustration (which are, like in the case of the first dimension, not central in the general design of Ukraine's vetting policy), as well as attempts to implement constitutional reform. Unlike the previous two dimensions, which fit into the general category of post-authoritarian transitional justice, this one refers to a post-conflict situation. The paradox in this dimension is the fact that the solution of the conflict is yet to come. In other words, within this dimension, transitional justice measures can become an instrument of peacemaking and peacebuilding.

In this dimension, the political component is dominant: a political agreement that will eventually bring an end to the conflict may define the shape of legal actions implemented to deal with the legacy of the conflict. Policies implemented within this dimension do not have an unequivocal impact on the political development of the state. On the one hand, there were attempts to avoid impunity for crimes committed by Ukrainian servicemen, which should be regarded as an indicator of reinforcing the rule of law principle, but simultaneous concessions to the self-proclaimed "people's republics" induced the perception of such actions as unjust. Additionally, the draft amendment of the constitution proposed by President Poroshenko opened the way for a *de facto* introduction of two separate legal orders within the borders of the same country. Generally, this dimension of transitional justice is the most open-ended: while the conflict is ongoing, any transitional justice measures undertaken are nothing more than a "trying out" process, a mere argument in negotiations over the future post-conflict settlement.

In an attempt to sum up the overall impact of the whole package of transitional justice policies on the political development of Ukraine, one can state the following. Neither of the analysed dimensions of transitional justice has led to an observable decrease in the level of patrimonialisation of the state or an improvement within the field of rule of law. On the contrary, its insufficient delivery can be regarded as one of the reasons for a further decrease in public trust in state institutions. This occurs despite the fact that there are cases where the policies have actually achieved positive results. The scale of delivery, however, remains too small to alter the society's perception of actual change, both in terms of quantity (the amount of vetted officials) and quality (the fact that there are no "big names" on the lists of those clearly affected by the transitional justice policies, putting aside the prohibition for the leaders of the Opposition Block to hold public positions under the lustration law, the effects of which can become more "visible" for ordinary citizens only when the political party they represent comes to power). The prominent exception from this rule is presented by the police – the reform preceded by vetting has led to an obvious increase in public trust in this institution, although this change appeared to be insufficient to alter the general assessment of the situation in the country.

An accurate assessment of the first two years of transitional justice in Ukraine requires distinguishing between initiating and implementation of transitional justice policies. As was mentioned in the particular chapters of the book, the majority of the policies have been initiated soon after the instalment of the post-Euromaidan interim government. It would be correct to say that the main motivation of the authorities to do so was the high demand from the side of the society: indeed, the concept of "dealing with the past" and "rebooting the political system" dominated the public debate in the first weeks after the Euromaidan. However, they were expressed primarily by a relatively narrow group of so-called opinion-makers. There is no clear evidence that these issues were equally significant from the perspective of the whole *demos*. As a result, it is the narrow group of activists who have become the main drivers and proponents of transitional justice policies, in particular of vetting and historical justice, but also of investigations and trials. As later measurements of public opinion have shown, Ukrainian citizens predominantly do not care about specific transitional justice policies. In other words, most transitional justice policies were initiated at a period of uncertainty, the representatives of the new regime had no true image of societies' expectations regarding how to "deal with the past". Taking into account that the consolidation of democracy has been declared the "normative anchor" of the new regime, it was rational to open up to the demands of the most active part of the society, which declared an attachment to the same values and additionally participated in the most violent uprising in post-1991 history of Ukraine.

When it comes to implementation, the generally well-designed policies started faltering, especially after a realisation that the implementation of particular transitional policies will not necessarily improve electoral prospects. In the circumstances of the ongoing destabilisation of the country after the annexation of Crimea and the rise of the "people's republics" in Donbas, the authorities became much more sensitive to the interests of powerful oligarchs and their representatives in the state apparatus who in fact appeared to be the main addressees of transitional justice policies. As a result, this post-Euromaidan dimension of transitional justice became a victim of Ukraine's widespread problem of selective law enforcement. A good comment of this situation is provided by a popular joke: "The severity of laws is compensated by the lack of obligation to implement them".

It was different in the case of the Donbas-related dimension of transitional justice policies. The conflict evolved steadily and the authorities had much better possibilities to measure societies' expectations. As a result, the emphasis by the Ukrainian authorities is put on a peaceful resolution of the conflict. There is no evident attempt to develop a comprehensive vision about how transitional justice in a post-conflict arrangement may look like; the measures undertaken in this field were limited to reactions on the most evident cases where the law was broken.

The insufficient delivery of transitional justice is also the result of a lack of coordination between the different dimensions of transitional justice. To a large extent, this can be explained by the unexpected emergence of an extremely significant issue (the Donbas conflict), the urgency of which has breached the pace of the transitional justice measures oriented more or less towards the distant past. Hence, the ongoing conflict obviously constitutes the most urgent, existential problem of the state. Due to the need to face unprecedented security threats, the military was practically excluded from the lustration policy. On the other hand, the criminal prosecution of *Berkut* officers forced many of them to escape to Russia; one can also assume that these prosecutions had an impact on decisions of at least a part of police officers in Donbas to support the emerging "people's republics". The need to introduce constitutional amendments as a result of the Minsk agreements has also provided an informal "security shield" for the judges of the CCU, protecting them from lustration. Tetiana Kozachenko, the head of lustration department in the Ministry of Justice has publicly criticized the president for not firing judges falling under the provision of the lustration law.[21] Keeping the

21 'Holovnyy lyustrator doriknula Poroshenkovi nezvilnennyam suddiv KS', *Ukrayinska Pravda*, 21 March 2016, http://www.pravda.com.ua/news/2016/03/21/7102800/ (accessed 17 May 2016).

judges in "suspension" together with criminal prosecutions against them as a part of post-Euromaidan investigations and trials obviously creates the possibility to exert influence on their decision. At the same time, if judges understand their necessity to produce "right" decisions in crucial issues, it opens the way for their acting in their own interest, such as maintaining uncertainty about the ultimate fate of the lustration law, which to a large extent hampers the whole vetting policy. Last but not least, Ukraine's new historic policy may be used by the propaganda of Russia and the "people's republics" to sabotage the peace process and raise the stakes in peace negotiations.

Most transitional justice policies implemented in post-Euromaidan Ukraine present a predominantly prospective, rather than retrospective, logic. Dealing with the past in this case means not "revenge" on the *ancien regime*, but rather an instrument of overcoming significant structural problems of the state's political system. It would be correct to say that the very fact of initiating transitional justice policies provides an indicator that the 2014 transition is not a mere replacement of the political elites accompanied by a modification of political regime, as it was in 2004 and to some extent in 2010. In particular, it is an indicator of the strength of civil society organisations opting for the development of Ukraine towards the direction proclaimed by the post-Euromaidan authorities. On the other hand, the failure to deliver concrete results proves that the discussed policies have not become an expected factor supporting the evolution of the political system in that direction. This happened primarily due to unfavourable external (from the perspective of transitional justice policies) political and economic factors. Generally speaking, the case of Ukraine proves Geoff Dancy's argument that "stable democratic practice and peace are subject to equifinality, that is, they are the product of many simultaneously operating processes. Demonstrating that the proceedings of a three-year truth commission or the passage of one amnesty law lead to democracy, stripped of every other factor changing during the transition, is nearly impossible".[22]

It should be explicitly stressed here that these conclusions are far from being final. They refer to the initial phases of transitional justice in Ukraine. Further research in this field is clearly needed and more fundamental conclusions will be able to be drawn with a more distant time perspective.

22 Geoff Dancy, 'Impact Assessment, Not Evaluation: Defining a Limited Role for Positivism in the Study of Transitional Justice', *The International Journal of Transitional Justice*, vol. 4 (2010), 367.

Taking into account what we know about the evolution of demand of Ukraine's public opinion, it is possible to foresee two dimensions of transitional justice finding their development in the following years. The first one obviously refers to the Donbas conflict. A thoughtful transitional justice policy dealing with the legacy of the conflict may help establish the rule of law in the course of post-Euromaidan transition of Ukraine. A lack of it would almost inevitably create new social tensions regardless on how the final resolution of the conflict will look like. The second dimension will most likely focus on the economic crimes, especially corruption. Within this field, one can expect a more innovative approach to transitional justice policies. However, it may diffuse with other anti-corruption measures. The main distinguishing feature will be the same as defined at the beginning of the book: whether the eventual anti-corruption measures will focus more strongly on the pre-Euromaidan period and whether the logic of treating large-scale corruption and economic crimes committed by the country's leadership as structural violence (the foundations of which have already been established). Within these two dimensions, the domestic demand for the implementation of transitional justice measures will correspond with international pressure: The Donbas conflict is already a subject of negotiations within the wider international setting and one should also not forget about the possibility of the ICC engaging in investigation of the situation. The fight against corruption is in turn one of the main expectations of those providing of international financial support, crucially needed by Ukraine's weak economy.

Finally, the discussed case of transitional justice in post-Euromaidan Ukraine presents a new pattern of policies of dealing with the past in post-communist countries. The discussed transitional justice instruments are not designed to address the communist past directly. Instead, the basic philosophy beyond these instruments can be defined as an attempt to fix the shortcomings of the initial phases of democratic consolidation, which eventually lead to tragic outcomes – the bloody culmination of the Euromaidan protest and the armed conflict in Donbas. In other words, Ukraine in recent years has created an interesting precedent of transitional justice targeted against the ones who abused the establishment and consolidation of democracy after the initial transition of 1991. Importantly, the design of the involved instruments suggest that they are primarily thought of as the ones dealing with the violation of law within the same political and legal order, reinforcing other legal instruments (such as the fight against corruption, protection of state sovereignty, etc.). Therefore, they basically do not face the problem of retrospective justice. What leads us to think about these instruments as going beyond the framework of normal justice is the extraordinary political situation and scale of problems faced by Ukraine. Dealing with them effectively, undoubtedly, requires going beyond the logic of pure "legal justice" and adding political elements to it. One should also remember that a *façade* of democratic institutions and the games of the oligarchic clans behind them are not exclusively Ukrainian feature of politics. More countries in the post-Soviet space (one may look at Moldova or Georgia) may try to deal with similar "aberrant periods" of their transitions, repeating Ukraine's post-Euromaidan experience.

Bibliography

Books and articles

1. 'Hromadyanska reaktsiya na falsyfikatsiyu rezultativ vyboriv i politychnu kryzu', *Natsionalna bezpeka i oborona*, no. 10 (2004): 13.
2. 'Prychyny, shcho obumovlyuyut' neobhidnist' provedennya administratyvnoyi reformy v Ukrayini', *Natsionalna bezpeka i oborona*, no. 5 (2000).
3. Ambrosio, Thomas, 'Beyond the Transition Paradigm: A Research Agenda for Authoritarian Consolidation', *Demokratizatsiya*, Vol. 22, No. 3 (2014).
4. Andrieu, Kora, 'An Unfinished Business: Transitional Justice and Democratization in Post-Soviet Russia', *The International journal of Transitional Justice*, Vol. 5 (2011).
5. Arnould, Valerie and Chandra Lekha Sriram, 'Pathways of Impact: How Transitional Justice Afects Democratic Institution-Building', *TJDI Policy Paper*, no. 1 (2014).
6. Aslund, Anders and Michael McFaul (ed.), *Revolution in Orange: The Origins of Ukraine's Democratic Breakthrough*, (Washington D.C.: Carnegie Endowment for International Peace, 2006).
7. Aslund, Anders, *Ukraine. What Went Wrong and How to Fix It*, (Washington D.C.: Peterson Institute for International Economics, 2015), 4.
8. Bachmann, Klaus and Igor Lyubashenko (ed.), *The Maidan Uprising, Separatism and Foreign Intervention. Ukraine's complex transition*, (Frankfurt am Main: Peter Lang Edition, 2014).
9. Bachmann, Klaus, 'Ukraine's Transitional Challenges. The Traps and Pitfalls in the Wake of the Maidan Protests', *Centre for International Relations Comments and Opinions*, no. 1 (2014).
10. Banchuk, Oleksandr, 'Chomu suddi masovo ponovlyuyut zvilnenyh politseyskyh, i yak tse zupynyty', *Ukrayinska Pravda*, 05 May 2016.
11. Bell, Christine, 'Transitional justice, Interdisciplinarity and the State of the "Field" or "Non-Field"', *The International Journal of Transitional Justice*, Vol. 3 (2009).
12. Berezovets, Taras, *Aneksiya: ostriv Krym. Hroniky 'hibrydnoyi viyny'*, (Kyiv: Brayt Buks, 2015).
13. Berman, Ilan, 'Closing the Archives. What Russia's Renewed Secrecy Says About Putin', *Foreign Affairs*, 24 April 2016.
14. Bielousov, Iurii L. et al., *Surviving Hell: Testimonies of Victims on Places of Illegal Detention in Donbas*, (Kyiv: TsP Komprint, 2015).

15. Buckley, Michael, 'The Priority of Legitimacy in Times of Political Transition', *Human Rights Review*, no. 14 (2013).
16. Carothers, Thomas, 'The End of the Transition Paradigm', *Journal of Democracy*, Vol. 13, No. 1 (2002).
17. Carranza, Ruben, 'Plunder and Pain: Should Transitional Justice Engage with Corruption and Economic Crimes?', *The International Journal of Transitional Justice*, vol. 2 (2008).
18. Cohen, Josh, 'The Historian Whitewashing Ukraine's Past', *Foreign Policy*, 2 May 2016.
19. D'Anieri, Paul, *Understanding Ukrainian Politics. Power, Politics and Institutional Design*, (New York, London: M.E. Sharpe, 2007), 13–14.
20. Daly, Erin, 'Truth Scepticism: An Inquiry into the Value of Truth in Times of Transition', *The international Journal of Transitional Justice*, Vol. 2, 2008.
21. Dancy, Geoff, 'Impact Assessment, Not Evaluation: Defining a Limited Role for Positivism in the Study of Transitional Justice', *The International Journal of Transitional Justice*, vol. 4 (2010).
22. de Greiff, Pablo and Roger Duthie (ed.), *Transitional Justice and Development. Making Connections*, (New York: Social Science Research Council, 2009).
23. Denisova, Oksana, 'Chto na tom beregu?', *Zerkalo Nedeli*, 22 January 2016.
24. Desyatnikova, Irina, Irina Kotsina, Aleksandr Shvets, 'Viktor Shokin: K sozhaleniyu, u mnogih nashih sotrudnikov, kak ya govoryu, v glazah tolko dollary', *Fakty*, 17 October 2015.
25. Duthie, Roger, 'Introduction,' in *Justice as Prevention. Vetting Public Employees in Transitional Societies*, ed. Alexander Mayer-Riekh and Pablo de Greiff, (New York: Social Science Research Council, 2007).
26. Elster, Jon, *Closing the Books. Transitional Justice in Historical Perspective*, (Cambridge: Cambridge University Press, 2004).
27. Engstrom, Par, 'Transitional Justice and Ongoing Conflict', in *Transitional Justice and Peacebuilding on the Ground. Victims and ex-combatants*, ed. Chandra Lekha Sriram et al., (London and New York: Routledge, 2013).
28. Eristavi, Maxim, 'Now We Know Who Really Runs Ukraine', *Foreign Policy*, 17 February 2016.
29. Flikke, Geir, 'Pacts, Parties and Elite Struggle: Ukraine's Troubled Post-Orange Transition', *Europe-Asia Studies*, Vol. 60, No. 3 (2008).
30. Freeman, Mark, *Necessary Evils. Amnesties and the Search for Justice*, (New York: Cambridge University Press, 2009).
31. Fukuyama, Francis, *Political Order and Political Decay: From the Industrial Revolution to the Globalization of Democracy*, (London: Profile Books, 2014).

32. Fukuyama, Francis, *The Origins of Political Order: From Prehuman Times to the French Revolution*, (London: Profile Books, 2012).
33. Galtung, Johan, 'Violence, Peace, and Peace Research', *Journal of Peace Research*, Vol. 6, No. 3 (1969).
34. Garcia-Godos, Jemima and Chandra Lekha Sriram, 'Introduction', in *Transitional Justice and Peacebuilding on the Ground. Victims and ex-combatants*, ed. Chandra Lekha Sriram et al., (London and New York: Routledge, 2013).
35. Gissel, Line Engbo, 'Justice Tides: How and When Levels of ICC Involvement Affect Peace Processes', *The International Journal of Transitional Justice*, no. 9 (2015).
36. Hecht, Lisa and Sabina Michalowski, 'The Economic and Social Dimension of Transitional Justice', https://www.essex.ac.uk/tjn/documents/Theeconomicandsocialdimensionsof TJ.pdf.
37. Horne, Cynthia M., 'The Impact of Lustration on Democratization in Post-communist Countries', *The International Journal of Transitional Justice*, Vol. 8 (2014).
38. Horne, Cynthia M., 'Transitional Justice and Social Trust in Post-Communist Countries', *Warsaw East European Review*, vol. III (2013).
39. Hrycak, Jarosław, *Nowa Ukraina. Nowe interpretacje*, (Wrocław: College of Eastern Europe, 2009).
40. Huntington, Samuel, *The third wave. Democratization and the late twentieth century*, (Norman: University of Oklahoma Press, 1991).
41. Jović, Dejan, 'Problems of Early Post-Communist Transition Theory: From Transition from to Transition to', *Politička misao*, Vol. 47, No. 5 (2010).
42. Judt, Tony, 'The "Problem of Evil" in Postwar Europe', *The New York Review of Books*, February 2008.
43. Kozak, Tetiana, 'Good Riddance to Bad Rubbish?', *Transitions Online*, 20 October 2014.
44. Kuchma, Leonid, *Ukrayina – ne Rossiya*, (Moscow: Vremya, 2003), 123.
45. Kuybida, Roman, 'Pravo na spravedlyviy sud: inshi aspekty', in *Prava lyudyny v Ukrayini: pershe pivrichchya 2015*, ed. Alla Blaga and Oleg Martynenko (Kyiv: Ukrayinska helsinska spilka z praw lyudyny, 2015).
46. Kuzio, Taras, 'Impediments to the Emergence of Political Parties in Ukraine', *Politics*, vol. 34 no. 4 (2014).
47. Leshchenko, Sergii, 'Why I'm Pessimistic about Ukraine's New Government', weblog on Atlantic Council, 20 April 2016, http://www.atlanticcouncil.org/blogs/new-atlanticist/why-i-m-pessimistic-about-ukraine-s-new-government (accessed 16 May 2016).

48. Leshchenko, Sergii, *Mezhyhirskyy syndrom. Diagnoz vladi Yanukovycha*, (Kyiv: Brayt Buks, 2014).
49. Letki, Natalia, 'Lustration and Democratisation in East-Central Europe', *Europe-Asia Studies*, Vol. 54, No. 4 (2002).
50. Lytvynenko, Oleksandr, 'Ideya pidvyshchennya samostiynosti rehioniv Ukrajiny w konteksti vyborchoyi kampaniyi', *Natsionalna bezpeka i oborona*, no. 11 (2004).
51. Markowski, Radosaw et al., *Democratic Audit of Poland 2014*, (Frankfurt am Main: Peter Lang Edition, 2015).
52. Matsiyevski, Yuri, 'Change, Transition, or Cycle. The Dynamics of Ukraine's Political Regime in 2004–2010', *Russian Politics and Law*, Vol. 49, No. 5 (2011).
53. Matuszak, Sławomir, *The Oligarchic Democracy. The influence of business groups on Ukrainian politics*, (Warsaw: Centre for Eastern Studies, 2012).
54. Mayer-Rieckh, Alexander, 'On Preventing Abuse: Vetting and Other Transitional Reforms', in *Justice as Prevention. Vetting Public Employees in Transitional Societies*, ed. Alexander Mayer-Riekh and Pablo de Greiff, (New York: Social Science Research Council, 2007).
55. Motyl, Alexander J., *Dilemmas of Independence: Ukraine after Totalitarianism*, (New York: Council of Foreign Relations Press, 1993).
56. Nalepa, Monika, *Skeletons in the Closet. Transitional Justice in Post-Communist Europe*, (New York: Cambridge University Press, 2010).
57. O'Brien, Thomas, 'Problems of political transition in Ukraine: leadership failure and democratic consolidation', *Contemporary Politics*, vol. 16, no. 4 (2010).
58. O'Donnell, Guillermo and Philippe C. Schmitter, *Transition from Authoritarian Rule. Tentative Conclusions about Uncertain Democracies*, (Baltimore and London: The Johns Hopkins University Press, 1986).
59. Oleinikova, Olga, 'Beyond Two Decades of Social Transition in Ukraine: The Underestimated Power of Agency in Transition Research', *Australian and New Zealand Journal of European Studies*, vol. 5 (2013).
60. Olsen, Tricia D., Leigh A. Payne, Andrew G. Reiter, *Transitional Justice in Balance. Comparing processes, weighing efficacy*, (Washington D.C.: United States Institute of Peace Press, 2010).
61. Olszański, Tadeusz A., 'Aftermath of the Maidan. Ukrainian society two years after the revolution', *Centre for Eastern Studies Commentary*, 04 March 2016.
62. Olszański, Tadeusz A., 'The local government elections in Ukraine', *Centre for Eastern Studies Analyses*, 04 November 2015.

63. Pettai, Eva-Clarita and Vello Pettai, *Transitional and Retrospective Justice in the Baltic States*, (Cambridge: Cambridge University Press, 2015).
64. Pierson, Paul, 'Increasing Returns, Path Dependence, and the Study of Politics', *The American Political Science Review*, vol. 94, no. 2 (2000).
65. Popova, Maria, *Politicized Justice in Emerging Democracies. A Study of Courts in Russia and Ukraine*, (New York: Cambridge University Press, 2014).
66. Przeworski, Adam, 'Institutions Mater?', *Government and Opposition*, vol. 39, no. 4 (2004).
67. Rahmanin, Sergey, 'Glava MVD Arsen Avakov: "My zdes vse ne svyatye"', *Zerkalo Nedeli*, 12 February 2016.
68. Ramsbotham, Oliver, Tom Woodhouse and Hugh Miall, *Contemporary conflict resolution: the prevention, management and transformation of deadly conflicts*, 3rd ed. (Cambridge, Malden: Polity Press, 2011).
69. Rapatsa, Mashele, 'Transformative Constitutionalism in South Africa: 20 Years of Democracy', *Mediterranean Journal of Social Sciences*, vol. 5, no. 27 (2014).
70. Rieff, David, *In Praise of Forgetting. Historical Memory and Its Ironies*, (New Haven and London: Yale University Press, 2015).
71. Rustow, Dankwart A., 'Transitions to Democracy: Toward a Dynamic Model', *Comparative Politics*, Vol. 2, No. 3 (1970).
72. Ryabchuk, Mykola, *Ulyublenyy pistolet Pani Simpson. Khronika pomaranchevoyi porazky*, (Kyiv: K.I.S., 2009).
73. Sharp, Dustin N., 'Emancipating Transitional Justice from the Bonds of the Paradigmatic Transition', *International Journal of Transitional Justice*, no. 9 (2015), 150–169.
74. Sharp, Dustin N., (ed.), *Justice and Economic Violence in Transition*, (New York: Springer, 2014).
75. Sheremet, Pavel and Sevgil Musayeva-Borovyk, 'Serhiy Horbatyuk: My blyzki do zavershennya spravy Mezhyhirya', *Ukrayinska Pravda*, 19 February 2016.
76. Shibalov, Evgeny, 'DNR iznutri. Kratkiy likbyez', *Zerkalo Nedeli*, 26 September 2014.
77. Shporlyuk, Roman, *U poshukah maybutnioho chasu*, (Kyiv: Hrani-T, 2010), 21.
78. Skaaning, Svend-Erik, 'Political Regimes and Their Changes: A Conceptual Framework', *CDDRL Working Papers*, No. 55 (2006).
79. Snyder, Timothy, *Black Earth: The Holocaust as History and Warning*, (New York: Tim Duggan Books, 2015).

80. Stan, Lavinia and Nadya Nedelsky (ed.), *Post-Communist Transitional Justice. Lessons from Twenty-Five Years of Experience*, (New York: Cambridge university Press 2015).
81. Stan, Lavinia, 'Determinants of Post-Communist Transitional Justice: An Overview', paper prepared for the Global Challenges Conference "Justice and Imagination: Building Peace in Post-Conflict Societies", Mount Holyoke College, 28 February–1 March 2014.
82. Studenna-Skrukwa, Marta, *Ukraiński Donbas. Oblicza tożsamości regionalnej*, (Poznań: Wydawnictwo Nauka i Innowacje, 2014).
83. Syroid, Oksana, 'Eshche raz ob osobennostyah "osobennostyey samoupravleniya" ', *Zerkalo Nedeli*, 15 January 2016.
84. Teitel, Ruti G., *Transitional Justice*, (New York: Oxford University Press, 2000), 223.
85. Tomak, Mariya, 'Zwilneni terytoriyi Donbasu: pravoohorontsi ignoruyut' zlochyny boyovykiv?', 03 October 2015, http://www.radiosvoboda.mobi/a/27256092.html (accessed 19 February 2016).
86. Tsebelis, George, *Veto Players: How Political Institutions Work*, (Princeton: Princeton University Press, 2002).
87. Volkov, Aleksey, 'Lyustratsiya ili kastratsiya?', *Zerkalo Nedeli*, 29 May 2015.
88. Vyatrovych, Volodymyr, 'Vozvrashchaem lyudyam istoriyu, istorii vozvrashchaem lyudey', *Zerkalo Nedeli*, 1 April 2016.
89. Waldorf, Lars, 'Just peace? Integrating DDR and transitional justice', in *Transitional Justice and Peacebuilding on the Ground. Victims and ex-combatants*, ed. Chandra Lekha Sriram et al., (London and New York: Routledge, 2013).
90. Wegner, Patrick, 'Regional and Local Perceptions of Justice and their Impact on International Investigations', in *The Legacy of Crimes and Crises. Transitional Justice, Domestic Change and the Role of the International Community*, ed. Klaus Bachmann and Dorota Heidrich, (Frankfurt am Main: Peter Lang Edition, 2016).
91. Wilson, Andrew, 'Survival of the Richest: How Oligarchs Block Reform in Ukraine', *European Council on Foreign Relations Policy Brief*, April 2016, 6.
92. Wilson, Andrew, *The Ukrainians: Unexpected Nation*, (New Haven and London: Yale University Press, 2002).
93. Wilson, Andrew, *Ukraine Crisis: What It Means for the West*, (New Haven and London: Yale University Press, 2014).
94. Wilson, Andrew, *Ukraine's Orange Revolution*, (New Haven: Yale University Press, 2005).

95. Wilson, Andrew, *Virtual Politics: Faking Democracy in the Post-Soviet World*, (New Haven, London: Yale University Press, 2005).
96. Wolczuk, Kataryna, *The Moulding of Ukraine: The Constitutional Politics of State Formation*, (Budapest: Central European University Press, 2001).
97. Yanevsky, Danylo, *Khronika 'Pomaranchevoyi' revolutsiyi*, (Kharkiv: Folio, 2005).
98. Zakrievskaya, Yevgieniya, 'Obratnaya storona ochevidnosti', *Zerkalo Nedeli*, 18 December 2015.
99. Zięba, Marta, 'To what extent is lustration an effective mechanism of transitional justice and democratic consolidation? The case of Poland', *Security and Human Rights*, no. 2 (2012).

Documents

1. Civic Lustration Committee, *Rik lyustratsiyi v Ukrayini: istoriya peremoh ta sabotazhu*, (Kyiv, 2015).
2. Decree of the Cabinet of Ministers of Ukraine 'On creation of the Ukrainian Institute of National Memory', no. 764, adopted 31 May 2006.
3. Decree of the Cabinet of Ministers of Ukraine 'On preparation and publishing of a series of books "Rehabilitated by History"', no. 530, adopted 11 September 1992.
4. Decree of the Cabinet of Ministers of Ukraine 'Some issues related to the Ukrainian Institute of National Memory', no. 684, adopted 12 November 2014.
5. Decree of the President of Ukraine 'On optimisation of the system of executive bodies', no. 1085/2010, 9 December 2010.
6. Decree of the President of Ukraine 'The issue of the Ukrainian Institute of National Memory', no. 1086/2010, 9 December 2010.
7. Decree of the Presidium of the Verkhovna Rada of Ukraine, 'On preparation of the multi-volume scientific documentary publication on the victims of political repressions in Ukraine', no. 2256-XII, adopted 6 April 1992.
8. Decree of the Verkhovna Rada of Ukraine, 'On reacting to facts of breaking the oath of judge by judges of the Constitutional Court of Ukraine', no. 775-VII, adopted 24 February 2014.
9. Decree of the Verkhovna Rada of Ukraine, 'On the text of the Constitution of Ukraine in the wording of 28 June 1996, as amended and supplemented by the laws of Ukraine of 8 December 2003 no. 2222-IV, of 1 February 2011 no. 2952-VI, of 19 September 2013 no. 586-VII', no. 750-VII, adopted 22 February 2014.

10. Draft law 'On amendments to the constitution of Ukraine (as to justice)', no. 3524, registered 25 November 2015.
11. Draft law 'On amnesty for persons who at the time of committing crime took part in the anti-terrorist operation', no. 4519, registered 25 April 2016.
12. Draft law 'On amnesty in 2016', no. 4255, registered 17 March 2016.
13. Draft law 'On avoiding prosecution and punishment of persons participating in the events in Donetsk and Luhansk oblasts', no. 5082, registered 16 September 2014.
14. Draft law 'On carrying out lustration in Ukraine', no. 4570-3, registered 08 April 2014.
15. Draft law 'On carrying out lustration in Ukraine', no. 4570, registered 26 March 2014.
16. Draft law 'On certain restrictions on access to positions in the institutions of state authority of Ukraine', no. 7028-1, registered 04 February 2005.
17. Draft law 'On lustration in Ukraine', no. 4570-1, registered 08 April 2014.
18. Draft law 'On lustration in Ukraine', no. 4570-2, registered 08 April 2014.
19. Draft law 'On lustration', no. 7028-2, registered 02 March 2005.
20. Draft law 'On lustration', no. 7028, registered 01 February 2005.
21. Draft law on amendments to the Constitution of Ukraine (on decentralisation), no. 2217a, registered 01 July 2015.
22. Draft law on amendments to the Constitution of Ukraine (on justice), no. 3524, registered 25 November 2015.
23. European Commission for Democracy through Law, 'Opinion on the constitutional situation in Ukraine', no. CDL-AD(2010)044, 20 December 2010.
24. European Commission for Democracy through Law, 'Opinion on the Temporal Validity of Draft Transitional Provision 18 of the Constitution of Ukraine', no. CDL-AD(2015)030, 23–24 October 2015.
25. European Commission for Democracy through Law (Venice Commission), Final Opinion on the Law on Government Cleansing (Lustration Law) of Ukraine, Venice 19 June 2015, Opinion no. 788/2014.
26. European Commission for Democracy through Law, 'Final opinion on the law on government cleansing (Lustration law) of Ukraine', no. CDL-AD(2015)012, 19 June 2015.
27. European Commission for Democracy through Law, 'Joint Interim opinion on the law of Ukraine On the condemnation of the Communist and National Socialist (Nazi) regimes and prohibition of propaganda of their symbols', no. CDL-AD(2015)041, 21 December 2015.

28. General Assembly of the United Nations, 'Commemoration of the sixtieth anniversary of the end of the Second World War', no. A/RES/59/26, 3 May 2008.
29. Human Rights Watch, 'Ukraine: Fear, Repression in Crimea. Rapid Rights Deterioration in 2 Years of Russian Rule', 18 March 2016, https://www.hrw.org/news/2016/03/18/ukraine-fear-repression-crimea.
30. International Advisory Panel, 'Report of the International Advisory Panel on its Review of the Maidan Investigations', 31 March 2015.
31. International Criminal Court, The Office of the Prosecutor, 'Report on Preliminary Examination Activities 2014", 02 December 2014.
32. International Criminal Court. The Office of the Prosecutor, 'Report on Preliminary Examination Activities (2015)', 12 November 2015.
33. Law of Ukraine 'Criminal Code of Ukraine', no. 2341-III, adopted 5 April 2001.
34. Law of Ukraine 'On a restoration of trust in the judicial power in Ukraine', no. 1188-VII, adopted 08 April 2014.
35. Law of Ukraine 'On amendment to the Law of Ukraine "On government cleansing" regarding additional measures to ensure the defence capability of the state', no. 132-VIII, adopted 27 January 2015.
36. Law of Ukraine 'On amendments to the Constitution of Ukraine (on justice),' no. 1401-VIII, adopted 02 June 2016.
37. Law of Ukraine 'On amendments to the Criminal Code of Ukraine on the abuse of power by the military officials', no. 290-VIII, adopted 07 April 2015.
38. Law of Ukraine 'On application of amnesty in Ukraine', no. 392/96, adopted 01 October 1996.
39. Law of Ukraine 'On commemoration of the victory over Nazism in the Second World War', no. 315-VIII, adopted 9 April 2015.
40. Law of Ukraine 'On government cleansing (lustration)', no. 1682-VII, adopted 16 September 2014.
41. Law of Ukraine 'On Holodomor of 1932–1933 in Ukraine', no. 376-V, adopted 28 November 2006.
42. Law of Ukraine 'On National Anti-corruption Bureau of Ukraine', no. 1698-VII, adopted 14 October 2014.
43. Law of Ukraine 'On National Police', no. 580-VIII, adopted 2 July 2015.
44. Law of Ukraine 'On prevention of corruption', no. 1700-VII, adopted 14 October 2014.
45. Law of Ukraine 'On special order of local self-government in certain areas of Donetsk and Luhansk oblasts', no. 1680-VII, adopted 16 September 2014.

46. Law of Ukraine 'On the access to archives of the repressive bodies of the Communist totalitarian regime of 1917–1991', no. 316-VIII, adopted 9 April 2015.
47. Law of Ukraine 'On the condemnation of communist and national-socialist totalitarian regimes in Ukraine and prohibition of promotion of their symbols', no. 317-VIII, adopted 9 April 2015.
48. Law of Ukraine 'On the judicial system and the status of judges', no. 1402-VIII, adopted 02 June 2016.
49. Law of Ukraine 'On the legal status and commemoration of the memory of fighters for the independence of Ukraine in the twentieth century', no. 314-VIII, adopted 9 April 2015.
50. Law of Ukraine 'On the principles of state anti-corruption policy of Ukraine (Anti-corruption strategy) in 2014–2017', no. 1699-VII, adopted 14 October 2014.
51. Law of Ukraine 'On the Public Prosecutor's Office', no. 1697-VII, adopted 14 October 2014.
52. Law of Ukraine 'On the rehabilitation of victims of political repressions in Ukraine', no. 962-XII, adopted 17 April 1991.
53. Law of Ukraine 'On the right to a fair trial', no. 192-VIII, adopted 12 February 2015.
54. Law of Ukraine, 'On avoidance of prosecution and punishment of persons because of events that occurred during peaceful gatherings, and annulment of some laws of Ukraine', no. 743-VII, adopted 21 February 2014.
55. Report 'Rosyjskie zbrodnie wojenne we wschodniej Ukrainie w 2014 roku', http://www.donbasswarcrimes.org/raport/.
56. Resolution of the Parliamentary Assembly of the Council of Europe, 'Measures to dismantle the heritage of former communist totalitarian systems', no. 1096 (1996), adopted 27 June 1996.
57. Statement of the Verkhovna Rada of Ukraine on recognition by Ukraine of jurisdiction of the International Criminal Court on crimes against humanity and war crimes committed by the high officials of the Russian Federation and leaders of terrorist organisations "DNR" and "LNR", which have led to serious consequences, and mass murder of Ukrainian citizens, no. 145-VIII, adopted 4 February 2015.
58. Statement of the Verkhovna Rada of Ukraine to the International Criminal Court on recognition by Ukraine of jurisdiction of the International Criminal Court on crimes against humanity committed by top state officials, which have led to serious consequences, and mass murder of Ukrainian citizens during

peaceful protests in the period from 21 November 2013 to 22 February 2014, no. 790-VII, adopted 25 February 2014.
59. The International Federation for Human Rights, 'The price of Freedom. Summary of the public report of human rights organizations on crimes against humanity committed during the period of Euromaidan', 23 February 2015.
60. The International Federation for Human Rights, *Eastern Ukraine. Civilians caught in the crossfire*, October 2015, no. 667a.
61. United Nations Office of the High Commissioner for Human Rights, 'Report on Human Rights Situation in Ukraine, 16 May–15 August 2015', 8 September 2015.
62. United Nations, 'The Rule of Law and Transitional Justice in Conflict and Post-Conflict Societies: Report of the Secretary-General', S/2004/616, 23 August 2004.

Websites (sources of data)

1. Democratic Initiatives Foundation: http://dif.org.ua
2. Information Centre "Maidan Monitoring": http://maidan.org.ua
3. International Republican Institute: http://www.iri.org
4. Kyiv International Institute of Sociology: http://www.kiis.com.ua
5. Razumkov Centre: http://www.razumkov.org.ua
6. United Nations: http://www.un.org
7. World Justice Project: http://worldjusticeproject.org

Websites (institutions)

1. Amnesty International: https://www.amnesty.org
2. Civic Lustration Committee: http://lku.org.ua
3. Constitutional Court of Ukraine: http://ccu.gov.ua
4. Freedom House: https://freedomhouse.org
5. Government of Ukraine: http://www.kmu.gov.ua
6. High Council of Justice of Ukraine: http://www.vru.gov.ua
7. Human Rights Watch: https://www.hrw.org
8. International Centre for Transitional Justice: https://www.ictj.org
9. International Criminal Court: https://www.icc-cpi.int
10. International Renaissance Foundation: http://www.irf.ua
11. Judicial Reform Council: http://jrc.org.ua
12. Ministry of Justice of Ukraine: https://minjust.gov.ua
13. North Atlantic Treaty Organisation: http://www.nato.int

14. President of Ukraine: http://www.president.gov.ua
15. Prosecutor General's Office of Ukraine: http://www.gp.gov.ua
16. Security Service of Ukraine: http://www.sbu.gov.ua
17. State Archival Service of Ukraine: http://www.archives.gov.ua
18. Transparency International Ukraine: http://ti-ukraine.org
19. Ukrainian Institute of National Memory: http://www.memory.gov.ua
20. Verkhovna Rada of Ukraine: http://rada.gov.ua
21. Worldwide Movement for Human Rights: https://www.fidh.org

Websites (media outlets)

1. *Fakty* newspaper: http://fakty.ua/
2. *Hromadske TV*: http://hromadske.ua
3. *Livyy Bereg* web portal: http://lb.ua
4. New York Times newspaper: http://www.nytimes.com
5. Reuters news agency: http://www.reuters.com/
6. *Televiziyna Sluzhba Novyn* (TSN): http://tsn.ua
7. *Tyzhden* magazine, http://tyzhden.ua/
8. *Ukrayinska Pravda* online newspaper: http://www.pravda.com.ua
9. *Ukrinform* news agency: http://www.ukrinform.ua
10. UNIAN news agency: http://www.unian.ua
11. *Zerkalo Nedeli* newspaper: http://zn.ua

Studies in Political Transition

Edited by Klaus Bachmann

Vol. 1 Klaus Bachmann: Vergeltung, Strafe Amnestie. Eine vergleichende Studie zu Kollaboration und ihrer Aufarbeitung in Belgien, Polen und den Niederlanden. 2011.

Vol. 2 Klaus Bachmann / Thomas Sparrow-Botero / Peter Lambertz: When Justice Meets Politics. Independence and Autonomy of *Ad Hoc* International Criminal Tribunals. 2013.

Vol. 3 Kim Christiaens / Idesbald Goddeeris / Magaly Rodríguez García (eds.): European Solidarity with Chile 1970s-1980s. 2014.

Vol. 4 Klaus Bachmann / Igor Lyubashenko (eds.): The Maidan Uprising, Separatism and Foreign Intervention. Ukraine´s complex transition. 2014.

Vol. 5 Klaus Bachmann / Dorota Heidrich (eds.): The Legacy of Crimes and Crises. Transitional Justice, Domestic Change and the Role of the International Community. 2016.

Vol. 6 Klaus Bachmann: Der Bruch. Ursachen und Konsequenzen des Umsturzes der Verfassungsordnung Polens 2015-2016. 2016.

Vol. 7 Igor Lyubashenko: Transitional Justice in Post-Euromaidan Ukraine. Swimming Upstream. 2017.

www.peterlang.com

www.ingramcontent.com/pod-product-compliance
Ingram Content Group UK Ltd.
Pitfield, Milton Keynes, MK11 3LW, UK
UKHW061932100926
8556IPUK00007B/876

9 783631 671498